THE MEMORY OF WATER

BY
SHELAGH STEPHENSON

★

★

DRAMATISTS
PLAY SERVICE
INC.

THE MEMORY OF WATER
Copyright © 1999, 1997, Shelagh Stephenson

ALL RIGHTS RESERVED

SPECIAL NOTE

SPECIAL NOTE ON SONGS AND RECORDINGS

For Eoin O'Callaghan, with love

THE MEMORY OF WATER was produced by Manhattan Theatre Club (Lynne Meadow, Artistic Director; Barry Grove, Executive Producer) in New York City, on October 15, 1998. It was directed by John Tillinger; the set design was by James Noone; the costume design was by Jess Goldstein; the lighting design was by Donald Holder; the sound design was by Aural Fixation; and the production stage manager was Leila Knox. The cast was as follows:

MARY	J. Smith-Cameron
VI	Robin Moseley
TERESA	Suzanne Bertish
CATHERINE	Seana Kofoed
MIKE	David Hunt
FRANK	Peter McRobbie

THE MEMORY OF WATER received its premiere at the Hampstead Theatre, London, England, on July 11, 1996. It was directed by Terry Johnson; the set design was by Sue Plummer; the lighting design was by Robert Bryan; and the sound design was by John A. Leonard. The cast was as follows:

MARY	Haydn Gwynne
VI	Mary Jo Randle
TERESA	Jane Booker
CATHERINE	Matilda Ziegler
MIKE	Alexander Hanson
FRANK	Dermot Crowley

THE MEMORY
OF WATER

ACT ONE

Blackness. A pool of bluish-green light reveals Vi, aged around forty. She is sitting at a dressing table. The drawer is open. She wears a green taffeta cocktail frock circa 1962. She is sexy, immaculately made-up, her hair perfectly coiffed. She wears earrings and a matching necklace, and carries a clutch bag, from which she takes a cigarette and lighter. She lights up. The pool of light opens up to reveal the rest of the room in a dim, golden, unreal glow: a bedroom, dominated by a double bed in which Mary lies, wearing a pair of sunglasses. She watches Vi. The room is slightly old-fashioned, with dressing table and matching wardrobe. Some clothes are draped over a chair. There is a long diagonal crack running across the wall behind the bed. An open suitcase lies on the floor, half unpacked, a half-full bottle of whiskey and a pile of books on the bedside table.

MARY.   What do you want?

VI.   Someone's been going through these drawers.

MARY.   Not me.

VI.   What did you think you'd find?

MARY.   Nothing. *(She closes the drawer and looks over to the bed.)*

VI.   That crack's getting worse. Have you noticed anything about the view?

MARY. No.

VI. It's closer.

MARY. What is?

VI. The sea. Fifty yards closer. It'll take the house eventually. All gone without a trace. Nothing left. And all the life that happened here, drowned, sunk. As if it had never been.

MARY. D'you remember a green tin box with chrysanthemums on it?

VI. No.

MARY. It had papers in it. It's gone. Where is it?

VI. I've no idea.

MARY. What have you done with it? *(Vi picks up some books from the bedside table and looks through the titles.)*

VI. *Head Injuries and Short Term Changes in Neural Behaviour ... The Phenomenology of Memory ... Peripheral Signalling of the Brain. (She puts them down.)* Bloody hell, Mary. What's wrong with Georgette Heyer? *(Go to black. Fade up bedside lamp. Vi has gone. Mary is lying prostrate. She stirs and gets out of bed, goes to the dressing table, opens drawers, rifles through them. The phone rings.)*

MARY. Hello? ... What time is it? ... I wouldn't be talking to you if I was, would I? I'd be unconscious ... Where are you? ... Jesus ... you're what? So will you want me to pick you up from the station? *(The door opens and Teresa comes in.)*

TERESA. Oh ...

MARY. Hold on ... *(To Teresa.)* It's not for you.

TERESA. Who is it?

MARY. *(To caller.)* What? She's gone where? ... OK, OK. I'll see you later. Are you sure you don't want me to pick you up — *(She's cut off.)* Hello? ... Shit.

TERESA. Who was that?

MARY. A nuisance caller. We struck up a rapport.

TERESA. He's not staying here, is he?

MARY. Who?

TERESA. I'm presuming it's your boyfriend.

MARY. How much sleep have I had? *(She picks up a portable alarm clock and peers at it.)*

TERESA. How's his wife?

MARY. Jesus. Two and a half hours. *(She flops back on the pillows. Looks at Teresa.)* Why are you looking so awake?

TERESA. I've been up since quarter past five. Presumably he's leaving her at home, then.

MARY. You've got that slight edge in your voice. Like a blunt saw.

TERESA. I'm just asking —

MARY. Of course he's bloody leaving her at home. She's gone to stay with her mother.

TERESA. I thought she was ill.

MARY. Maybe she went in an iron lung. Maybe she made a miracle recovery. I don't know. I didn't ask.

TERESA. Where's he going to sleep?

MARY. What?

TERESA. You can't sleep with him in that bed.

MARY. He's staying in a hotel.

TERESA. I thought it might be something important.

MARY. What?

TERESA. The phone. Funeral directors or something.

MARY. We've done all that. Can I go back to sleep?

TERESA. And where's Catherine?

MARY. She said she might stay over with someone.

TERESA. Does she still have friends here?

MARY. Probably. I don't know. *(She turns away, settles down, and shuts her eyes. Teresa watches her for a while.)*

TERESA. She could have phoned to say. Anything could have happened to her. It's still snowing.

MARY. She's thirty-three, Teresa.

TERESA. The roads are terrible.

MARY. She'll get a taxi.

TERESA. Probably just as well she didn't come home. She'd have probably drunk four bottles of cider and been brought home in a police car. And then she'd have been sick all over the television.

MARY. She was thirteen when she did that.

TERESA. She was lucky she didn't get electrocuted.

MARY. It wasn't switched on.

TERESA.   Yes it was, I was watching it. It was *The High Chaparral.*
MARY.   No it wasn't. I wish you'd stop remembering things that didn't actually happen.
TERESA.   I was there. You weren't. *(Mary gives up trying to sleep. Sits up.)*
MARY.   I was there.
TERESA.   That was the other time. The time when she ate the cannabis.
MARY.   That was me. I ate hash cookies.
TERESA.   It was Catherine.
MARY.   It was me.
TERESA.   I was there.
MARY.   So where was I?
TERESA.   Doing your homework probably. Dissecting frogs. Skinning live rabbits. Strangling cats. The usual.
MARY.   Teresa. I'd like to get another hour's sleep. I'm not in the mood, OK? *(She tries to settle down in the bed, and pulls something out that's causing her discomfort: a glass contraption with a rubber bulb at one end. She puts it on the bedside table and settles down again. Teresa picks it up.)*
TERESA.   Oh, for God's sake ... Is this what I think it is?
MARY.   I don't know. What d'you think it is?
TERESA.   A breast pump.
MARY.   I found it on top of the wardrobe. I think I'd like to have it.
TERESA.   Why?
MARY.   Because you've got the watch and the engagement ring.
TERESA.   For Lucy. Not for me. For Lucy.
MARY.   OK. So you want the breast pump. Have it.
TERESA.   I don't want it.
MARY.   Good. That's settled. Now let me go to sleep.
TERESA.   You can't just take things willy-nilly.
MARY.   You did.
TERESA.   Oh, I see. I see what this is about. *(Mary sits up.)*
MARY.   It's not about anything, it's about me trying to get some sleep. For Christ's sake Teresa, it's too early in the morning for this. *(Mary pulls the covers over her head. Silence. Teresa goes to the door, turns back.)*

8

TERESA. Could you keep off the phone, I'm waiting for Frank to ring and my mobile's recharging —

MARY. If you take that phone to the funeral this time —

TERESA. Oh, go to sleep. *(Mary sits up.)*

MARY. I'm surprised Dad didn't burst out of his coffin and punch you.

TERESA. I didn't know it was in my bag.

MARY. You could have turned it off. You didn't have to speak to them.

TERESA. I didn't speak to them.

MARY. You did. I heard you. You told them you were in a meeting.

TERESA. You're imagining this. This is a completely false memory.

MARY. All memories are false.

TERESA. Mine aren't.

MARY. Yours in particular.

TERESA. Oh, I see, mine are all false but yours aren't.

MARY. That's not what I said.

TERESA. And what's with the Ray-Bans? *(Mary takes them off.)*

MARY. I couldn't sleep with the light on.

TERESA. You could have turned it off.

MARY. I was frightened of the dark.

TERESA. When did this start?

MARY. It's all right for you. You're not sleeping in her bed.

TERESA. Oh, for goodness' sake.

MARY. You grabbed the spare room pretty sharpish.

TERESA. I was here first.

MARY. Have the sheets been changed?

TERESA. Yes.

MARY. When?

TERESA. What difference does it make?

MARY. I don't like sleeping in her bed, that's all.

TERESA. She didn't die in it.

MARY. She was the last person in it. It's full of bits of skin and hair that belong to her —

TERESA. Stop it —

MARY. And it makes me feel uncomfortable —

TERESA. What bits of skin and hair?

MARY. You shed cells. They fall off when you're asleep. I found a toenail before.

TERESA. Please.

MARY. I thought I might keep it in a locket round my neck. Or maybe you'd like it —

TERESA. Stop it, for goodness' sake. *(Teresa picks up a book from the bedside table.)* You can't leave work alone for five minutes, can you, even at a time like this?

MARY. I've a very sick patient.

TERESA. You had a very sick mother.

MARY. Don't start, Teresa.

TERESA. Oh, she never complained. Because your job's important. I mean, doctors are second to God, whereas Frank and I only have a business to run, so obviously we could drop everything at a moment's notice.

MARY. It's not my fault. *(Silence.)*

TERESA. Why do we always do this?

MARY. What?

TERESA. Why do we always argue?

MARY. We don't argue, we bicker.

TERESA. OK, why do we bicker?

MARY. Because we don't get on.

TERESA. Yes we do.

MARY. Oh, have it your own way. *(She unscrews the whiskey and takes a swig. Teresa looks at her, aghast.)*

TERESA. You haven't even got out of bed yet.

MARY. It's the only way we're going to get through this. *(She offers it to Teresa, who shakes her head.)*

TERESA. D'you often have a drink in the morning?

MARY. Of course I bloody don't, what d'you think I am?

TERESA. Lots of doctors are alcoholics. It's the stress.

MARY. Someone dies, you drink whiskey. It's normal, it's a sedative, it's what normal people do at abnormal times. *(She takes another swig. Silence.)* OK. Let's be nice to each other. *(Silence.)* What do people usually talk about when their mother's just died?

TERESA. I don't know. Funeral arrangements. What colour

10

coffin. I've got a list somewhere.

MARY.   There should be a set form. Like those books on wedding etiquette. Sudden Death Etiquette. Lesson One. Breaking the news. Phrases to avoid include: guess what?

TERESA.   I was distraught, I wasn't thinking properly —

MARY.   I thought you'd won the lottery or something —

TERESA.   It's quite tricky for you, being nice, isn't it?

MARY.   Sorry. I forgot. How are you feeling? *(Teresa looks at her watch.)*

TERESA.   I was expecting him to phone an hour ago.

MARY.   I'm not talking about Frank.

TERESA.   I don't know how I feel. Everything I eat tastes of salt. *(Silence. Teresa crosses the room and takes the whiskey from Mary. She takes a swig and grimaces.)* Salt. Everything tastes of it. *(Hands it back. Sits on the bed.)* The funeral director's got a plastic hand.

MARY.   God. *(Pause.)* What's it like?

TERESA.   Pink.

MARY.   What happened to his real one?

TERESA.   How should I know?

MARY.   Didn't you ask him?

TERESA.   It didn't seem appropriate.

MARY.   No. I suppose not.

TERESA.   He was showing us pictures of coffins.

MARY.   As they do.

CATHERINE.   *(Off.)* Hi!

MARY.   Oh God.

TERESA.   In here. *(Catherine bursts in, wrapped in layers of coats and scarves, laden with carrier bags. She divests herself as she speaks.)*

CATHERINE.   God, it's bloody freezing out there. It's like *Scott of the Antarctic*, the cab was sliding all over the place and I had one of those drivers who kept saying, have you been shopping, are you going somewhere nice? And I said, yes, actually, a funeral. My mother's. I thought, that'll shut him up, but it turns out he knew her. I forgot what it's like up here. Everyone knows the butcher's daughter's husband's mother's cat. And he got all upset, we had to pull over, so anyway I invited him to the funeral. He's called Dougie. I bet he doesn't come. God, I've got this really weird pain at the very bottom of my stomach, here, look, just above my pubic bone. It keeps going sort of stab, twist, so either I've got some sort of cyst, but actually, God, I know what it is, I bet. I bet I'm ovulating. Isn't that amazing? I can actually feel the egg being released. Although, hang on, I don't think I'm due to ovulate. You can't ovulate twice in the same month, can you? It's not my appendix because I haven't got one. Fuck. It must be PMT. In which case I think I've got an ovarian cyst. *(Silence.)*

MARY.   D'you want us to take you to hospital or shall I whip it out now on the kitchen table?

CATHERINE.   I'll be fine.

MARY.   Good, because I'm over the limit for either activity.

CATHERINE.   Oh brilliant, whiskey. *(She picks up the bottle and takes a slug.)*

TERESA.   Where've you been?

CATHERINE.   Shopping.

TERESA.   Shopping?

CATHERINE.   Well, you'd call it a displacement activity, but I call it shopping.

TERESA.   All night?

CATHERINE.   I went for a drink. I stayed with some friends.

TERESA.   What friends?

CATHERINE.   You don't know them. Oh God, there it goes again. Have you ever had this? Right here. Right at the bottom of your stomach?

TERESA.   No.

CATHERINE.   What d'you think it is?

MARY.   I've no idea.

TERESA.   We've been worried sick.

CATHERINE.   Look, just here — *(She takes Mary's hand and holds it against her groin.)*

MARY.   Wind.

CATHERINE.   Do any of your patients actually survive?

TERESA.   You could have picked up a phone. I mean, where've you been?

CATHERINE.   Down the docks shagging sailors, what d'you think?

MARY.   I'd have come with you if I'd known.

TERESA. It's just a bit insensitive —

MARY. Yes it is. There's a time and a place for everything —

TERESA. Disappearing, leaving us to deal with all this —

CATHERINE. All what? D'you like my shoes? I can't stop buying shoes. I even like the smell of them. Honestly, it's just like an eating disorder except it's not it's just shoes although sometimes it's underwear. D'you ever get that, you have to buy twenty pairs of knickers all at once, usually when you're a bit depressed —

TERESA. You can't wear those for a funeral. You look like Gary Glitter.

CATHERINE. I didn't buy them for the funeral.

MARY. I remember them the first time round. They were horrible then.

CATHERINE. I got them in a sale.

MARY. Oh well. That's some consolation.

CATHERINE. What's wrong with them?

TERESA. I thought you didn't have any money.

CATHERINE. Credit cards. What's wrong with them?

TERESA. You said you were broke.

CATHERINE. Oh, for God's sake, broke doesn't mean you can't buy things. I'm trying to cheer myself up, or is that not allowed? The minute I walk in the door I feel it in waves, the two of you waiting to pounce, looking for something to criticize. Christ, it's no wonder I've got low self-esteem.

MARY. You have an ego the size of Asia Minor.

CATHERINE. I'm just asking you to clarify your position *vis-à-vis* my shoes. I mean, quite obviously you don't like them, but why d'you always have to do this sneery superior thing? Why can't you just be straight and say you hate them?

MARY. I hate them. Can I go back to sleep now?

TERESA. I'm just wondering how you can afford to go out and buy all this stuff if you haven't got any money.

MARY. She shoplifts.

CATHERINE. Will someone tell me what I'm supposed to have done?

MARY. It was a joke.

CATHERINE. So all right, I know, Mum's dead —

TERESA.   There's no need to put it like that —

CATHERINE.   But you want me to sit down and cry about it and I can't.

MARY.   I don't. I want you to go away.

CATHERINE.   You always do this to me.

MARY.   I'm tired.

CATHERINE.   Some of the things you say to me are just, you know, not on. It's like I don't count. All my bloody life. And I'm not having it anymore. I won't take it any more, OK?

TERESA.   Have you been taking drugs, Catherine?

CATHERINE.   Oh, for God's sake. I was in a really good mood till I walked in here.

TERESA.   Your mother's just died, how can you be in a good mood? Try and be a bit more sensitive —

CATHERINE.   No one's being sensitive to me.

MARY.   We fucking are! *(Silence.)*

CATHERINE.   Did Xavier call?

MARY.   Who?

CATHERINE.   Xavier.

MARY.   I thought he was called Pepe?

CATHERINE.   You see, this is what you do to me. This permanent, constant, endless belittling.

TERESA.   He didn't call.

CATHERINE.   I'm about to marry him and you can't even get his name right.

MARY.   You're always about to marry people.

CATHERINE.   What's that supposed to mean?

MARY.   And you never do.

TERESA.   Oh shut up, both of you. *(Silence.)*

CATHERINE.   If I don't get some pain killers I'm going to die.

MARY.   There might be some paracetamol in my case.

CATHERINE.   Haven't you got anything more exotic? *(Catherine goes to the suitcase.)*

MARY.   Not for you, no. They're in the pocket. Now, will you both go away and let me get some sleep?

TERESA.   Would anyone like some barley cup? *(Catherine finds the paracetamol and takes a couple.)*

CATHERINE.   I'd rather drink my own urine.

14

MARY. You may laugh.

TERESA. I do not drink my own urine.

MARY. Yet.

CATHERINE. Haven't we got any ordinary tea?

TERESA. That stuff in the kitchen's made from floor sweepings. You might as well drink liquid cancer.

MARY. God, you do talk absolute shite sometimes.

TERESA. Some people think that drinking your own urine —

MARY. Yes I know. And they're all mad.

TERESA. You're always so certain when it comes to things you know nothing about.

MARY. You know bugger all about bugger all.

TERESA. You've a completely closed mind, it infuriates me. You're so supercilious, you don't even listen —

MARY. If God had meant you to ingest your own urine, he'd have rigged up a drinking-straw arrangement directly from your bladder. To save you the indignity of squatting over a teacup. Now, please, I just want an hour.

TERESA. There are things to do.

MARY. They can wait.

CATHERINE. I'm going to have a hot bath and a joint. I can't stand this. *(She goes.)*

TERESA. So once again it's me. Everything falls to me.

MARY. Go and have a lie down, Teresa.

TERESA. I can't bloody lie down, I can't sit still. I can't cope, I need some Rescue Remedy. *(She goes out.)*

MARY. I've got some beta blockers, they're much better —

TERESA. *(Off.)* I get agitated. I get like this. I don't need drugs. *(She comes back, carrying her bag, chanting.)* Brown one-and-a-half pounds of shin of beef in a heavy casserole. Remove and set aside. Sauté two medium onions in the casserole with two crushed cloves of garlic —

MARY. What are you doing?

TERESA. Recipes. I recite recipes. It's very soothing. I've tried meditation but my mind wanders. I think of all the phone calls I should be making instead of sitting there going "om". Carbonnade of beef seems to work best.

MARY. You're a vegetarian.

15

TERESA. I've tried it with nut loaf but it's not the same. And now I've got that salt taste in my mouth and I feel sick.

MARY. Psychosomatic.

TERESA. I know it's psychosomatic. I know it is, all right. I'd just like it to stop, that's all. *(Catherine comes in with a bundle of mail.)*

CATHERINE. More fan mail.

MARY. I thought you'd gone for a bath to soothe your cyst.

CATHERINE. There's not enough water. So it's still sort of niggling, I wish it would stop — *(She goes to her carrier bags and takes out various pieces of clothing. She opens the wardrobe door, holds them up against herself in front of the mirror.)* I think it's stress. I mean it's an incredibly stressful time, isn't it, and I always get things like this when I'm strung out. Last year I had this weird thing in my legs, like they were kind of restless or jumpy or something. Every time I tried to go to sleep they used to sort of twitch and hop. The doctor in Spain said it was quite common and I just needed to relax more, but I can't, I've got an incredibly fast metabolism and then I get that spasm thing in my stomach which is definitely stress-related, I'm sure it's irritable bowel syndrome. I mean, that starts up the minute I'm even a tiny bit tense, I notice it straight away because I'm very in touch with my body, I can sort of hear it speaking to me. *(Pause.)*

TERESA. I think I'm going mad.

CATHERINE. Last night I dreamed I could do yogic flying. I bet that means something — *(She tugs at the jacket.)* I'm not sure about this, are you? I don't suit black, that's the problem.

TERESA. As soon as the phone went I knew.

CATHERINE. Can your wear trousers at a funeral?

TERESA. I said to Frank, I can't answer it. We should never have left her at the hospital like that. We should have stayed.

MARY. You weren't to know.

TERESA. I'm not good with hospitals, I had to get away. Everyone in her ward looked like they'd already died, everyone was pale grey with a catheter. *(Mary is opening the mail. Reads.)*

MARY. "With deepest sympathy on your sad loss, Mimi." Who's Mimi?

TERESA. When Frank spoke to them they said, she's worse, you'd better get up to the hospital. I took the phone and said, she's dead isn't she, you don't phone at three in the morning unless someone's dead. And then, this is the awful bit, I put the phone down, and the next thing I wanted to do more than anything else was have sex, which is sick, I know, that's what Frank said afterwards. I know I should have phoned you two, but I had this idea, this flicker she might not be dead, even though I knew she was really, but they wouldn't tell me over the phone, and I'd have woken you up, and what would the point be anyway, you were miles away —

MARY. It's OK. Stop worrying about it —

TERESA. That's why I didn't phone straight away. Mimi used to live three doors down.

CATHERINE. Can I borrow a skirt from someone?

TERESA. I keep going over and over it —

CATHERINE. Is anyone listening to me?

MARY. Oh, shut up and sit down. Your cyst might burst.

TERESA. And the doctor was about twelve, and embarrassed. Eventually we had to say it for him. He kept fiddling with his pen and giving us a rundown of everything that had happened, until eventually Frank said, "Are you trying to tell us she's not coming back? Are you trying to tell us she's dead?" And he said, "More or less, yes." And I said, what d'you mean, more or less? She's either dead or she isn't, you can't be a bit dead, for God's sake. And then I looked at my feet and I was wearing odd shoes. A black one and a brown one. Not even vaguely similar. So I started to laugh and I couldn't stop. They had to give me a sedative. Frank was shocked. They're not like us, his family, they've got Italian blood. Someone dies, they cry. They don't get confused and laugh.

CATHERINE. All I want to know is, can I borrow a skirt?

MARY. Oh shut up, Catherine, for Christ's sake!

CATHERINE. If I could get an answer out of anyone, I would —

MARY.   Yes, you can borrow a fucking skirt! *(Silence. Teresa goes to her bag and takes out a bottle of pills. She takes two.)*

CATHERINE.   What are they?

TERESA.   Nerve tablets. Have one, for heaven's sake. Have six. Have the lot. They're completely organic, no chemicals.

CATHERINE.   I like chemicals.

TERESA.   *(Emptying her bag on to the bed.)* All right, don't then. I've got a list somewhere. Things to sort out.

MARY.   Do it later Teresa.

TERESA.   I can't. I can't sit still. I have to do it now

MARY.   You're a useless advertisement for the health food industry.

TERESA.   Supplements. We do health supplements. Remedies. How many times do I have to tell you? You do this deliberately, you willfully misinterpret what we do because you think it's funny or something, and actually I'm getting bored with it.

CATHERINE.   You're making me incredibly tense, both of you.

TERESA.   We're making you tense? Good God, you haven't stopped since you came in. Jumping around all over the place like you're on speed, which, thinking about it, you probably are, blahing on about your ovaries and your restless legs and your PMT. I don't give a toss about your insides. Has anyone seen my electronic organizer? *(They look vaguely round the room. Silence.)*

MARY.   What does it look like?

TERESA.   I had it a minute ago, I had it — *(Teresa throws her bag down. Silence. Catherine offers her the joint.)*

CATHERINE. D'you want some of this?

TERESA.   No, thank you.

MARY.   Maybe you should.

CATHERINE.   It's completely organic. We grew it in the garden. *(Teresa takes a reluctant puff. Then another. Silence.)* You know when you went to the hospital. When she was dead ...

TERESA.   Mmmm ...?

CATHERINE.   Did you see her?

TERESA.   Who?

CATHERINE.   Mum.

TERESA. Of course I did.

CATHERINE. How did she look?

TERESA. Asleep. She just looked asleep. *(Catherine takes the joint back.)*

CATHERINE. Oh good. *(Silence.)*

TERESA. It's got the list on it. My organizer's got the list on it. *(Catherine opens an envelope and reads a card.)*

CATHERINE. "My thoughts are with you at this sad time. Your mother was a wonder woman. Norman Pearson." Norman Pearson? *(Teresa takes the card from her and looks at it.)*

TERESA. Patterson. Norman Patterson.

MARY. Who's he? And what does he mean "wonder woman"?

TERESA. I don't know. He's got an allotment.

CATHERINE. I'm starving. Is anyone else hungry?

MARY. Maybe they were having an affair.

CATHERINE. Munch munch munch, I'd really like some Shreddies. Have we got any Shreddies, d'you think?

TERESA. She was getting more and more confused. Everything was packing up. I wanted to take her to that herbalist in Whitby. She wouldn't have any of it.

MARY. I don't think the colonic irrigation was a very good idea. Not for Alzheimer's Disease.

TERESA. You don't know the first thing about colonics —

MARY. I do know that your colon is specifically designed to function independently, without recourse to a foot pump.

TERESA. She never took care of herself, that's the problem.

MARY. She was seventy-five. She died. Let her be.

TERESA. She still smoked.

MARY. So what?

TERESA. She died because her heart gave out because she never ever looked after herself properly.

MARY. I don't think that's strictly true.

TERESA. You're a doctor, you know it's true.

MARY. OK. It's all her own fault. She ate sliced white bread so she deserves to die. Whereas you wouldn't have it in the house, so you'll probably manage to avoid death altogether. That's the general idea, isn't it? While the rest of us deserve all we get,

19

because we've been recklessly cavalier in the diet department. Or we couldn't quite stomach six feet of plastic tubing being shoved up our bottoms —

TERESA.   Thank God you're not my doctor —

MARY.   Thank God you're not my patient —

TERESA.   I'm just saying, if you eat properly —

MARY.   And I'm just saying people die. You can't avoid it. Not even you.

TERESA.   Well, you two managed to avoid it pretty comprehensively when it came to Mum. Most of the time you weren't even here.

MARY.   Great. The guilt fest. I knew we'd get there eventually.

CATHERINE.   It's no good trying to make me feel guilty because I don't.

TERESA.   I didn't think for a moment you would.

CATHERINE.   You'd like me to, though, and I won't. I refuse. I've nothing to feel guilty about at all. I didn't like her.

MARY.   Who?

CATHERINE.   Mum.

TERESA.   Don't be ridiculous.

CATHERINE.   She didn't like me.

MARY.   Yes she did.

CATHERINE.   How do you know?

TERESA.   She was your mother.

CATHERINE.   I had a horrible childhood.

TERESA.   We all had the same childhood. It wasn't horrible.

CATHERINE.   Mine was.

MARY.   That's because you're an egomaniac.

CATHERINE.   She thought I was the menopause.

MARY.   Who told you that?

CATHERINE.   She did. She had the cat put down without telling me. She shut me in a cupboard. She said it was an accident but it wasn't.

MARY.   When did she do all this?

CATHERINE.   I never had the right shoes. She wouldn't let me visit you in the hospital when you had an exploding appendix. She did it deliberately. She excluded me from everything. She made me stay in the shop after closing time and count nails.

MARY.   When I think of our childhood, we went on a lot of bike rides and it was always sunny.

TERESA.   Well, it was for you. You couldn't put a foot wrong.

CATHERINE.   When I think of it, it was always pissing down. And what bike? I never had one.

TERESA.   I'm sure you came to the beach with us, I remember it —

CATHERINE.   The only time I went to the beach, it was with you and you left me there. You forgot me. You didn't remember till you got home and mum said, where's Catherine?

TERESA.   That was Mary. She was too young, she was being a pain and showing off in Esperanto, so we ran away and left her. With no bus fare and the tide coming in.

CATHERINE.   It was me!

MARY.   No it wasn't. It was me.

CATHERINE.   So how come I remember it?

MARY.   Because I told you about it and you appropriated it because it fits. If it was horrible, it must have happened to you. And she didn't have the cat put down, it just died.

TERESA.   It got run over by a combine harvester actually.

CATHERINE.   I don't remember any of this.

TERESA.   The amount of chemicals you've had through your system, I'm surprised you can remember anything at all.

CATHERINE.   You did leave me at the beach. Someone left me at the beach. I remember it vividly. I've got a brilliant memory. I remember everything.

TERESA.   You've forgotten Lucy's birthday every year since she was born —

MARY.   You'd go mad if you remembered everything. What would be the point? Your head would burst. There's an illness actually, a sort or incontinent memory syndrome, where you recall everything, absolutely everything, in hideous detail, and it's not a blessing, it's an affliction. There's no light and shade, no difference between the trivial and the vital, no editing system whatsoever. *(She looks at Catherine.)* Actually, Catherine, maybe you should come in for a few tests.

CATHERINE.   You're doing it again! *(Teresa has spied something under the bed. She picks it up: her electronic organizer.)*

TERESA.   I've found it. I've found my list. *(She consults the gadget.)* Insurance — undertakers 10.30, bridge rolls — I think there's just the flowers left —

CATHERINE.   Do we have to do this now?

TERESA.   It won't get done on its own. If it was up to you two, she'd have to cremate herself —

MARY.   All right, all right —

TERESA.   Because whilst you were doing Spanish dancing with Pepe in Fuengirola —

CATHERINE.   His name's Xavier and I've never been to Fuengirola in my life —

TERESA.   I was watching her fall apart. Twenty miles here, twenty miles back. Three times a week.

CATHERINE.   I spoke to her a week ago. She wasn't that bad. She said she was off to the hairdressers.

TERESA.   Oh, for goodness' sake, she was mad as a snake. And I'm the one who dealt with it all.

MARY.   I'm sure when they publish a new edition of *Foxe's Book of Martyrs* they'll devote a chapter entirely to you.

TERESA.   Every month something else went, another wire worked itself loose. Not big things, little things. She used to put her glasses in the oven. "What day is it?" she'd say, and I'd say, "Wednesday" and she'd say "Why?" "Well, it just is. Because yesterday was Tuesday." And she'd say "There was a woman here with a plastic bucket. Who is she?" "Elaine. You know Elaine. Your home help." And then she'd look at me and we'd start all over again. "What day is it?" I mean, she wasn't even that old. *(Silence. She takes some sheets of photographs from her bag.)* Anyway. I got these photos from the florist. There's a number under each picture, so if you just give me the number of the wreath you want, I can phone in the order. *(She hands the photos to Mary, who gives them a cursory glance.)*

MARY.   I'll have the one in the shape of a football.

TERESA. I'm just trying to keep things in a neutral gear, that's all.

MARY. Choosing flowers for your mother's funeral is not what I'd call a neutral activity. *(The phone rings. Teresa and Mary both make a grab for it. Mary wins.)* Hello? ... Hello?

CATHERINE. Is it Xavier?

MARY. Hello?

TERESA. Give it to me.

MARY. There's just a crackling sound. Hello, can you hear me? *(Teresa grabs the receiver.)*

TERESA. Frank?

CATHERINE. It'll be Xavier. *(Mary grabs it back.)*

MARY. Mike? *(The line goes dead. She puts the receiver down. Silence.)* It's like waiting for the relief of Mafeking. *(Silence.)*

CATHERINE. Does anyone want a sandwich? *(Mary gets out of bed and rifles through her suitcase for clothes. Catherine begins to go.)* I went to this brilliant funeral in Madrid — *(She goes out.)*

MARY. Brilliant. You went to a brilliant funeral.

CATHERINE. *(Off.)* He was a friend of Xavier's who fell off a roof and at the party afterwards they had little bowls of cocaine —

MARY. Oh, what a good idea. That'll go down well with the St. Vincent de Paul Society.

CATHERINE. *(Off.)* And they dyed his poodle black. Just for the funeral. It was washable dye so it wasn't cruel, but anyway, it was raining and God, you should have seen the state of the carpets afterwards. So that was a bit of a disaster, but later on there was a firework display and he went up in a rocket.

MARY. Who?

CATHERINE. *(Off.)* The person who was dead. Not the poodle.

MARY. We're not doing that to Mum. *(Catherine reappears in the doorway carrying a bread knife.)*

CATHERINE. I'm just saying that funerals don't have to be depressing. They can be quite happy.

MARY. Farcical even.

CATHERINE. Scrambled eggs. That's what I want. I bet we haven't got any eggs — *(Exit Catherine.)*

MARY. I keep having dreams about her.

TERESA. Who?

CATHERINE. Mum. *(Teresa opens a card.)*

TERESA. Thank God. I thought you meant Catherine. It's bad enough having her in the same house without dreaming about her as well.

MARY. She's about fortyish and she's always wearing that green taffeta dress.

TERESA. "With deepest sympathy from Winnie and the boys. Sorry we won't be able to make the funeral due to a hip replacement op."

MARY. I've never heard of any of these people, have you? And there's this smell in the dream.

TERESA. Can you dream smells?

MARY. I think so.

TERESA. I can't.

MARY. It was that perfume she used to wear. In a tiny bottle, she got it in Woolworth's, and on Saturday night when she leaned over to say good night, she smelt of cigarettes and face powder and something alcoholic, and this perfume.

TERESA. Phul Nana.

MARY. Phul Nana ... that was it ... the whole room smelt of it.

TERESA. She always said, if you don't wear perfume you'll never find a man.

MARY. You'll never get a boyfriend.

TERESA. And then, frankly —

MARY. Unless you're a nun.

TERESA. You might as well cut your throat with the bread knife.

MARY. I don't know how she managed to give birth to three daughters and then send us out into the world so badly equipped. She'd have sent us up K2 in slingbacks. With matching handbags.

TERESA. She must have taught us something, otherwise we'd all be dead. *(Pause.)* Did she ever mention sex to you? *(Mary gives her a withering look.)* No, I suppose not.

MARY. I found a box of sanitary towels in her wardrobe once. I was nine. I said, what are these? I mean, I knew they were something bad, but I was desperate, I dared myself to ask. I was thinking all sorts of things. She snatched the box off me and

24

said, "Put that back. It's a home perm kit." *(There is a banging noise at the window.)*

TERESA.   What was that?

MARY.   There's something at the window ...

TERESA.   Hello ...? *(The sound comes again.)* Oh God, it's like *Wuthering Heights.*

MARY.   Someone wants to come in.

TERESA.   Well, open the window.

MARY.   You do it.

TERESA.   Oh for goodness' sake — *(She goes to the window and opens it, screams.)*

MIKE.   Sorry ...

MARY.   Mike ... Oh Jesus ... Teresa, this is Mike ...

TERESA.   Hello.

MIKE.   I've been ringing the doorbell.

TERESA.   It's broken.

MARY.   Yes. *(Pause.)* I'd like to come in, if that's not too much trouble. Otherwise, you know, I could just stand here and die, apparently it's a nice way to go, freezing, you don't feel a thing, you just drift off into oblivion —

MARY.   Oh God, yes, sorry, I'll open the door —

MIKE.   For Christ's sake — *(He climbs in through the window, covered in snow.)*

MARY.   How long have you been there?

MIKE.   Hours.

MARY.   Sorry. Here, give me your coat.

TERESA.   We thought you were Heathcliff. At the window.

MIKE.   Drink. I need a drink.

MARY.   *(Taking off his outer clothes.)* Heathcliff wasn't at the window. He was inside. It was Cathy trying to get in.

MIKE.   Sorry?

TERESA.   Are you sure? *(Catherine appears, eating a sandwich and smoking another joint. She has a glass in her hand.)*

CATHERINE.   Who's this?

MARY.   Mike, this is Catherine. Catherine, this is Mike. *(He tries to smile.)*

MIKE.   Sorry, can't speak. Frozen.

CATHERINE.   Mike the married boyfriend Mike? *(Mary fetches the whiskey.)*

TERESA.   Would you like a cup of tea?

CATHERINE.   You don't look a bit like you do on the television. You're quite small really, aren't you?

MIKE.   People say this to me all the time, but I'm not actually.

CATHERINE.   Mind you, you'd never think Robert Redford was only five foot five, would you? *(Mary snatches the glass from Catherine.)*

MARY.   Give me that. *(Fills it and gives it to Mike.)*

CATHERINE. They always do this to me. So, how tall are you?

MIKE.   I'm five eleven.

CATHERINE.   Don't be ridiculous, I don't believe you. *(Teresa hisses at her.)*

TERESA.   Catherine ...

CATHERINE.   Sorry, would you like some drugs? *(She holds the joint out to him. Mike shakes his head.)* Are you not allowed?

MARY.   He doesn't. Come here, sit down. *(He sits on the bed and she rubs his hands, undoes his shoes and takes them off.)*

MIKE.   I think I've got frostbite.

CATHERINE.   I won't tell anymore. Or I'll say you did but you didn't inhale.

MIKE.   I'm sorry?

CATHERINE.   That's what celebrities usually say.

MARY.   He's not a celebrity, he's a doctor.

CATHERINE.   I saw your programme yesterday. That woman with the psoriasis. God. I thought you were really good.

MIKE.   Thank you —

CATHERINE.   But you don't want to be caught with a joint in your hand, do you? On top of everything else. You can't be a drug addict *and* be having an affair. Can you imagine the papers? "TV Doctor blew my mind says hospital consultant" —

MARY.   Catherine you're off your face —

TERESA.   Why don't you come with me and make some tea for everyone?

CATHERINE.   Our mother's just died.

MIKE.   I know. I'm very sorry. *(Catherine bursts into tears.)*

MARY. I'm sorry about this, Mike. Catherine, stop it —

CATHERINE. God, is no one allowed to show their feelings around here? I'm depressed, I've suffered a bereavement, it's normal to cry, for God's sake —

MARY. Go away, stop doing this —

MIKE. It's OK, it's OK, she's allowed to be unhappy —

CATHERINE. You see? It's only you two who are weird, you don't know what it's like —

TERESA. *(Storming out.)* That's it. I'm getting a gun. *(Catherine throws herself on the bed and howls.)*

CATHERINE. We're orphans ... *(Mike puts his arm around her. She holds on to him, puts her head in his lap.)* And I'm the youngest, I had them for less time than everyone else did ...

MARY. Catherine, get up off that bed and get out —

MIKE. She's OK, she can't help it, what's the matter with you?

MARY. And you shut up, you know nothing. Catherine, if you don't get out of here, so help me God, I'll brain you. *(Catherine gets up weakly, weeping. She manages to look tiny and pathetic. She turns as she gets to the door.)*

CATHERINE. I've got that pain again ...

MIKE. What pain? Where? *(She totters over to Mike and lifts her sweater up.)*

CATHERINE. Just here ...

MARY. There's nothing wrong with you.

CATHERINE. She keeps saying that to me — *(The phone rings. She stops weeping immediately, and grabs it.)* Hello? ... Xavier? ... Fuck ... OK ... OK ... You're where? OK, I'll tell her. *(She slams the phone down.)* It's bloody Frank ... *(She storms out and slams the door. Off.)* Teresa!

MARY. I'm sorry. I'm sorry. You have to just ignore her. You don't understand.

MIKE. Why are you being so horrible to her?

MARY. Where d'you want me to start?

MIKE. OK, OK, OK, come here — *(She puts her arms around him and they kiss. It grows passionate. Eventually she pulls away).*

MARY. This is my mother's bed.

MIKE. I know. Sorry. So.

MARY.   So.

MIKE.   How are you?

MARY.   Fine.

MIKE.   Good.

MARY.   Did you bring that paper I asked you for? (*Mike squirms apologetically.*)

MIKE.   I couldn't remember the title.

MARY.   "A Trophic Theory of Neural Connections." Why didn't you write it down?

MIKE.   I didn't think, I mean, I didn't realize you needed it that badly. I thought you'd have enough on your plate. I mean, it's ridiculous, it's an obsession. What's the big deal about this patient? You've seen post-traumatic amnesia before, it's not that unusual —

MARY.   It's not an obsession. I've got close to him, that's all.

MIKE.   How can you get close to someone who can't remember his own name?

MARY.   Forget it. I'll look up the paper when I get back. (*Pause.*) Everything all right at home?

MIKE.   The same, you know. (*Pause.*)

MARY.   Mike.

MIKE.   What?

MARY.   D'you love me?

MIKE.   Yes.

MARY.   Say it then.

MIKE.   I love you. Now you.

MARY.   Now I what?

MIKE.   Now you say it. That's the form.

MARY.   Oh, this is ridiculous.

MIKE.   You started it. (*Silence.*)

MARY.   So. She's better then?

MIKE.   Who?

MARY.   Chrissie.

MIKE.   No. Why? What d'you mean?

MARY.   I saw a photo of the two of you. In the hospital magazine. At a tombola, for Christ's sake. And there she was, large as life. Fit as a fiddle. And I thought, where's the intravenous drip?

28

What happened to her catheter? I suppose it spoilt the line of her dress, did it?

MIKE. Mary —

MARY. I'm sorry, I can't help it, it brings out something horrible in me. I mean you always give the impression she's at death's door, practically in an iron lung —

MIKE. Don't exaggerate —

MARY. I'm exaggerating? You said she could hardly walk. Well, forgive me, but either that picture's trick photography, or she's doing the shagging twist —

MIKE. She was feeling a bit better.

MARY. God, what's the matter with me? It's Catherine, she makes me want to kill people, and right now I want to kill your wife, which is irrational and I'm sorry.

MIKE. You're in shock.

MARY. I'm not in shock. But let me just say this: People don't get off their deathbeds for a tombola.

MIKE. I'm sorry I went o a party with my wife. I'm sorry she's not as ill as you'd like her to be. Perhaps you'd prefer her to be dead too. For fuck's sake, Mary. What d'you want me to say?

MARY. I feel humiliated! I've rationalized, I've philosophized, I've come to terms with the fact that I'm living in some nether world with different rules where we don't do Christmas, we don't do bank holidays, and if you die I'll be the last to find out. I accept this because your wife's supposed to be incapable of crossing the street on her own, and now I discover her hopping round a dance floor like a bag of ferrets. I know I'm not supposed to feel things like humiliation or fury or jealousy because they're irrational but sometimes I do, sometimes I just do, OK? *(Silence.)*

MIKE. I'm sorry. *(Pause.)* I think I've got hypothermia. Can I get into bed? I'll keep my clothes on.

MARY. She'd probably quite like the idea of a man in her bed. Get in. *(He gets into bed. She sits down on the chair.)*

MIKE. Don't stay over there. Come and sit with me.

MARY. I'm fine here.

MIKE. Come on. Please. I've come all this way. The heating

broke down on the train, the lights went, and just when we thought we were out of the woods, there were frozen points, and the buffet car ran out of food. We sat in the middle of nowhere and I started to worry about who we'd eat first if things got really out of hand. The man opposite me looked like Margaret Rutherford. I tried to imagine filleting him with a pocket penknife.

MARY. I'll sit on the bed. I'm not getting into it. *(She perches primly next to him. He kisses her. She brings her feet up, but pulls her mouth away from his. Lies next to him on top of the covers. He puts his arm round her.)* I'm sorry. This is making me very tense. It just feels weird.

MIKE. Sorry, sorry, sorry. *(He puts his hands behind his head.)*

MARY. He can't remember his own name actually.

MIKE. Who?

MARY. That patient. It's coming back in bits. If you show him a bike, he can ride it. He can't remember what it's called, that's all.

MIKE. I was talking to someone the other day who'd worked in this lab in France a few years back ... or maybe he knew someone who worked there, I can't remember. Anyway, they were doing these experiments with water, because they were researching the efficacy of homeopathy, and what they came up with after months and months of apparently stringent tests was that you can remove every last trace of the curative element from a water solution and it will still retain its beneficial effect. And they decided that this meant water was like magnetic tape. That water had memory. You can dilute and dilute and dilute, but the pertinent thing remains. It's unseen, undetectable, untraceable, but it still exerts influence. I mean they did a full range of tests. It wasn't just a shot in the dark. *(Pause.)* It's all complete bollocks, of course. Except ...

MARY. Except what?

MIKE. I've got an erection. *(Pause.)*

MARY. We can't. We absolutely can't.

MIKE. No.

MARY. It'll go away if we ignore it. *(He leans over and kisses her. After a while she pulls away and gets up. She walks about the room,*

picking up objects from the dressing table, putting them down.) Everything I look at makes me want to cry. I see these things and a life
unravels in front of my eyes. I can't sleep for remembering.
MIKE.   What? *(Pause. Mary is nervous.)*
MARY.   Can you feel nostalgia for something that never really
existed? I remember growing up here. I remember nightlights
and a doll's house. I can see them in my mind's eye. And I'm not
sure we had either. I find myself aching, longing for it. This half-
imagined childhood.
MIKE.   You want to be a child again? *(Pause.)*
MARY.   I want to go through it again. The light on the landing,
the bedtime stories. Even though I know some of the memories
aren't real. It's like I've hooked up to some bigger, general pic-
ture, and it *feels* so real I can taste it. *(Pause.)* I think I'm preg-
nant. *(Pause.)*
MIKE.   What?
MARY.   You heard me.
MIKE.   You can't be.
MARY.   I am.
MIKE.   You can't possibly be.
MARY.   I know I'm geriatric, but I'm not completely desic-
cated —
MIKE.   Hang on a minute, this is ridiculous —
MARY.   It's not ridiculous.
MIKE.   Have you done a test?
MARY.   No, but I feel very strange.
MIKE.   What d'you mean, strange?
MARY.   As in I'm-pregnant strange, what d'you think I mean?
MIKE.   I'm not going to believe this till you've done a test.
MARY.   I'm the size of a house. Look at me.
MIKE.   You always look like that, don't you?
MARY.   Observant. There's another thing you're not. *(Pause.)* I
feel weird.
MIKE.   You can't. You can't feel weird.
MARY.   Well, I do.
MIKE.   This is unreal. This is completely unreal. I don't believe
this is happening —

MARY. Stop getting in a state, will you?

MIKE. I'm not getting in a fucking state! *(Silence.)* What are you going to do?

MARY. What am *I* going to do? What happened to *we?*

MIKE. OK, OK, we.

MARY. Well I kind of hoped for the usual. You know, nine months' gestation followed by birth of something small and squalling. Preferably human. Or perhaps I'm asking for too much.

MIKE. Let's not panic about it, OK?

MARY. I'm not panicking. You are.

MIKE. I'm not. I'm not. I mean you're probably not. Pregnant.

MARY. I am. *(She climbs on the bed next to him and kisses him. Puts her hand on his groin.)* Brilliant. I'm pregnant. Instant detumescence. *(Silence.)*

MIKE. I think ... I don't think ... you know, I mean, the thing is, I'm trying to say —

MARY. It might make the papers, your wife will be humiliated, you can't cope and you're leaving me.

MIKE. No, that's not what I'm trying to say. *(Pause.)* You're sure you're pregnant?

MARY. Would you like it in writing?

MIKE. I have to tell you there's a problem here. The thing is. How can I put this? The thing is, it's not mine. I mean if you are, it's not mine —

MARY. Just run that past me again, will you?

MIKE. I've had a vasectomy. *(Silence.)*

MARY. What?

MIKE. I've had a vasectomy.

MARY. You've had a vasectomy.

MIKE. Yes. *(Silence.)*

MARY. When?

MIKE. Before I met you. *(She stares at him.)* I wanted to tell you. I was going to, and then ... it didn't seem important I suppose ...

MARY. It didn't seem important.

MIKE. No ... I mean ... I just ... You never ... I mean it never came up ... I thought you didn't want children. You never said. I thought, you know, you had a career and everything.

MARY. You've got a career. You've also got three children.

MIKE. I'm sorry. I'm sorry. Why didn't you say anything? Why didn't you tell me you wanted a child?

MARY. I'm thirty-nine, Mike. I'm thirty-nine. Didn't you ever think?

MIKE. I'm not a mind-reader. You never showed the slightest sign. You never even hinted. *(Pause.)*

MARY. I thought you'd leave me.

MIKE. You thought I'd leave you?

MARY. I thought you'd leave me if I said I wanted a child. *(The door opens and Teresa comes in carrying a lot of black bin liners.)*

TERESA. You're going to hate me for this — oh, for goodness' sake. *(Mary and Mike spring apart. Mary gets up.)*

MARY. We were just talking. *(Mike gets out of bed.)*

MIKE. Look, fully dressed — *(Catherine comes in with another joint.)*

CATHERINE. Oh God, have you two been in bed? That's disgusting.

MARY. What? Look, Mike and I are trying to have a conversation —

TERESA. We have to sort out her clothes.

CATHERINE. Why do we have to do it now? *(Teresa is already taking clothes out of the wardrobe.)*

TERESA. A friend of mine's sending a truck to Zimbabwe and I promised I'd have them ready this afternoon.

MARY. She's not even in her grave yet, and apart from that —

TERESA. If we wait until after the funeral, I'll get left with it all.

MARY. Teresa, listen —

TERESA. No. You listen. If it wasn't for me, nothing would ever get done. She'd be lying on the floor stoned out of her brains, you'd be having it off in our dead mother's bed and I'd be holding the fort —

CATHERINE. St. Teresa of Avila —

TERESA. Somebody has to be practical! Somebody has to be in charge, you two can live in chaos but I can't —

CATHERINE. What chaos? *(She is rifling though the clothing, holding frocks up in front of herself.)* What's this made of, d'you think? Is it silk?

MIKE. Maybe I should, you know —

MARY. Don't even think about it —

MIKE. Fine.

MARY. I'm in shock, I still can't believe you —

TERESA. The sooner we get this over with the better. Right. I've worked it out. We divide it into two lots. Crap and good stuff.

CATHERINE. The crap we send to the poor bastards in Zimbabwe —

TERESA. The crap we take to the dump.

CATHERINE. I quite like this. Can I have it? *(She holds up a dress in front of her and hands the joint to Teresa, who puffs at it absentmindedly as she sorts through the clothes.)*

MIKE. Um, what would you like me to do?

MARY. I don't know. Hang yourself. *(She picks up the whiskey and takes a slug.)*

MIKE. D'you think you should be drinking? I mean —

MARY. Just lie down and die, will you?

TERESA. Mike, you take these bags. This one for rubbish, this one for good stuff. We'll hand it to you, you pack it.

MIKE. Right. OK. This one rubbish, this one good stuff ... *(Teresa takes another armful from the wardrobe and throws it on the bed. Mary stands stricken, staring at it. Catherine is posing in mirrors, holding up frocks.)*

TERESA. Oh for goodness' sake, Mary. I know it's not a very nice job, but it has to be done.

MARY. OK, OK. *(She picks up some clothes dispiritedly. Catherine picks up a gaudy floral number.)*

CATHERINE. God, d'you remember this? What a mistake. *(She dances round with the dress in front of her.)*

TERESA. I think that can go in the crap pile.

CATHERINE. They might like it in Zimbabwe.

TERESA. She wore that terrible hat with it, d'you remember? *(Catherine scrabbles through the pile. She picks up a hat.)*

CATHERINE. Here it is, here it is — *(Teresa begins to giggle. She takes another puff of the joint.)*

34

MARY. Is this what you add up to? A wardrobe full of tat and three pelican children?

TERESA. Oh dear, I do feel lightheaded ... have some of this, Mary, it's all so much easier ... pure thingy ...

CATHERINE. Grass.

TERESA. Exactly, no chemicals. *(She takes one more draw and hands the joint to Mary. Catherine has put the hat on, and is draping the dress around her.)* Cousin June's wedding. 1969.

CATHERINE. It was horrible even then. D'you remember we didn't want to sit next to her in church.

MARY. Give it to me. *(Takes it, hands it to Mike.)* This is for the rubbish.

MIKE. Are you sure? Maybe we should have another bag for kind of in-betweens. *(Catherine snatches the dress back.)*

CATHERINE. No, no it's you, Mary, it's perfect — *(She holds it against Mary who throws it aside. Mike puts it in the rubbish. Teresa yells.)*

TERESA. Aargh, look at this — *(She pulls out a sixties cocktail frock from the pile on the bed. Catherine doubles up with laughter.)* She can't have worn this, surely.

CATHERINE. She did, I remember it, oh God, give it here. *(She takes the dress and begins to struggle out of her clothes.)*

MARY. Catherine, for Christ's sake —

CATHERINE. I'm wearing underwear. Anyway, he's a doctor, stop being such a pain — *(There is a great cry of triumph from Teresa, who has been rooting around in the pile.)*

TERESA. Yes! *(She brings out a wild pink dress, circa 1963.)* This was her Alma Cogan phase. Which I think, on reflection, I prefer to the crimplene phase that followed it.

MARY. Teresa, are we sorting out these clothes or not because I've got better things to do at the moment?

TERESA. I mean what was crimplene, was it a sort of by-product of formica? *(She is holding the dress up against her in front of the mirror.)*

MARY. Oh, this is ridiculous —

TERESA. Actually, margarine, you know, is a by-product of plastic. Or is it petrol? *(Catherine has got the dress on, and a hat.)*

CATHERINE. What d'you think? Is it me? *(Teresa laughs with stoned hysteria. Even Mike laughs.)*

MARY. And I don't know why you're laughing — *(The room is in chaos. Catherine and Teresa are unstoppable now. Catherine is trying on shoes, hats, lipstick. Earrings, anything.)*

TERESA. Turn away, Mike, turn away — *(She goes behind the wardrobe door.)*

MARY. I give up. Give that to me. *(She takes the rubbish sack from Mike and starts to stuff clothing into it.)* Who did it?

MIKE. What?

MARY. The operation. Who did the operation?

MIKE. Charlie Morgan. Why? *(She starts to laugh.)*

MARY. Charlie Morgan?

CATHERINE. Who's Charlie Morgan? Oh, look, I've found a hairpiece from before the Boers War. Look at this —

MIKE. Is there a problem with that?

MARY. No, no, no. Honestly. *(Teresa emerges from behind the wardrobe door, looks in the mirror.)*

TERESA. Oh God, what do I look like?

MIKE. So what's funny?

MARY. Charlie-whoops-I've-made-a-bit-of-a-hash-of-this-Morgan.

MIKE. Oh, for God's sake, that's a slanderous rumour, he's OK.

MARY. He's in a clinic at the moment. Drying out.

MIKE. He did me years ago. He was steady as a rock.

MARY. You didn't notice an overpowering smell of aftershave?

MIKE. Christ. He wasn't drinking it, was he?

TERESA. *(Scrabbling around in the bottom of the wardrobe.)* Where're those pink shoes?

MARY. He's about to be struck off —

CATHERINE. Oh, look at this —

MARY. Gross professional negligence, I think it was —

CATHERINE. Mary, this is you — *(She holds out the green dress which Vi wore at the beginning of Act One.)*

TERESA. Oh, put it on —

MIKE. Are you sure?

MARY. Give me some of that joint, Catherine — positive —

TERESA. D'you think I need a handbag with this?

MARY. I can't believe you went to Charlie Morgan. Did he give you a special price or something? *(Mary takes the dress and starts to struggle into it, giggling.)*

MIKE.   Are you making this up?

CATHERINE.   Go for it, Mary!

MARY.   Performing microsurgery when he was so drunk he had double vision.

MIKE.   I think you're exaggerating a bit —

MARY.   I am not —

CATHERINE.   You need bigger hair. Big, crispy hair.

TERESA.   Yes, you see, you didn't get shiny hair in those days, did you? Honestly, all that hairspray, think of the carcinogens. Now, d'you think this bag or this — *(She holds up two. Mary has got the frock on now.)*

MARY.   There. What d'you think?

CATHERINE.   You look dead like mum. *(Momentary silence, before they realize, then screeches of appalled laughter. Teresa and Catherine roll on the bed, clutch their sides. Wild, stoned hysteria, etc. Mary joins in. The door opens and Frank comes in, in his overcoat, carrying a suitcase.)*

FRANK.   What the fuck ...? *(Silence)*

TERESA.   Frank ...

FRANK.   What are you doing?

MARY.   We're sorting out mum's clothes ... *(Pause.)*

CATHERINE.   D'you think we're sick? *(Frank looks at his watch.)*

FRANK.   It's taken me fourteen hours to get here from Dusseldorf. I spent six of those sitting next to a woman from Carlisle who runs a puppet theatre for the deaf. She'd maroon hair and drank an entire bottle of gin whilst telling me about her alcoholic father who once bit the head off a chicken. She was wearing a dress that looked like a candlewick bedspread and she'd been on a course in Cologne learning mime and North African devil dancing. I thought, take me back to sanity. And I walk into this. Pan's bloody People. *(Silence. The women suppress their hysteria.)*

MIKE.   I'm Mike. Hi.

FRANK.   How d'you do. And then I got diverted to East Midlands.

MIKE.   Goodness.

FRANK.   What is it with this country? It's too hot, it's too cold, there's leaves on the line, it's the wrong sort of snow —

CATHERINE.   Frank, chill out, have some drugs — *(They all begin to giggle uncontrollably.)*

FRANK.   How long have they been like this?

MIKE.   I think it's grief, you know ... *(The women get more hysterical. They hold on to each other and look at themselves in the mirror. They scream with laughter.)*

MARY.   Oh God, what do we look like.

CATHERINE.   Where's my camera, where's my camera? *(She goes to her bag and scrabbles around. Pulls out a camera.)*

TERESA.   Oh yes, we've got to have a photo —

FRANK.   Don't be ridiculous —

CATHERINE.   Frank, you take it — *(She hands it to him. They all chant together like a football mob.)*

ALL.   Photo, photo, photo —

FRANK.   OK, OK ... *(The women chant and pose and laugh hysterically.)* Christ, they're a handful when they all get together. They just gang up, you'll get used to it ... all right, all right, pull yourselves together ... Where d'you want to be ...? *(They all line up in front of the bed, linking arms and staggering and pushing each other.)*

MARY.   OK, OK, smile everyone!

CATHERINE.   I want to be in the middle! *(They arrange and rearrange themselves. Frank takes a photo. A flash. Freeze frame: the women smiling in a row, arms linked. We realize there is a fourth person in the line-up: Vi, smiling, cigarette held aloft, in her green taffeta dress.)*

END ACT ONE

ACT TWO

Scene 1

Lights up on stage exactly as before: Mary and Vi are alone. Vi gives her a long look.

VI.   You look ridiculous in that.

MARY.   The tin with the chrysanthemums on it. The one you don't remember. Where is it?

VI.   I told you. I've no idea.

MARY.   What have you done with it?

VI.   You need a bit of colour on your face. You were always pasty.

MARY.   Don't change the subject. Where's the tin? *(Pause.)*

VI.   Have you tried the shed?

MARY.   No.

VI.   It might be in the shed.

MARY.   I'll look then.

VI.   Although it might not. It's been years since I saw that tin. It had toffees in it originally. From Torquay. I'd have liked to have gone there. They have palm trees. I've never seen a palm tree in real life. I expect you've seen dozens. You're probably sick to death of palm trees. *(Mary pulls on jeans and sweaters.)* I do wish you'd wear something more feminine occasionally.

MARY.   Apparently I look ridiculous. I'm going to look for the tin. *(She begins to go by Vi stops her.)*

VI. This patient. The one you've got all the books about. What's wrong with him?

MARY. He got hit on the head and lost his memory. *(Vi gives a soft laugh.)*

VI. So what's the prognosis? Doctor.

MARY. He'll recover. More or less intact. I think.

VI. Intact. I like that word. Intact. Everything in order. In the bag. Right as ninepence. That's nice. Was he in a fight?

MARY. No, he opened a cupboard and a jar fell on him.

VI. Must have been a big jar.

MARY. Pickled bell peppers.

VI. You wouldn't get pickled bell peppers up here. Probably a good thing. They sound dangerous.

MARY. Can I go now? *(Vi has taken a dress from the pile.)*

VI. Look. D'you remember this?

MARY. No.

VI. I loved this dress. It was the only dress your father ever bought me. *(She begins to dance. It's slightly seductive and sensuous.)* Saturday nights I used to wear this. The men loved me, you know. Oh yes. All the men loved me. And I loved the men. I never cared for the women. I never liked them. Once I got my first bra I couldn't be doing with them anymore.

MARY. Pity you had three daughters really, isn't it? *(Vi stops dancing.)*

VI. You put words into my mouth. Every one of you does it, but you in particular, you mangle everything into something else. My comedy mother. My stupid, bigoted, ignorant mother.

MARY. Well you shouldn't say such stupid things.

VI. You lie in bed with your lovers and you tell stories about me. None of them complimentary. Most of them complaining. None of them true.

MARY. Excuse me. I'm going to look for that tin. *(She turns to go.)*

VI. Don't walk away from me! You've done that all your life. *(Mary turns round, like a guilty child. Vi picks up a book from the bedside table and opens it at random. Reading.)* "A biological memory system differs from a simple information storage device, by virtue of its inherent ability to use information in the service of its own survival ... A library, for example, couldn't care less about its own survival. The problem is not one of storage. The problem is the difference between a dead and a living system." *(She shuts it.)* So there's a difference between a cat and a bookcase. I could have told you that. *(She looks at the price on the back of the book.)* Twenty-five ninety-nine. My God. *(Puts it down.)* I don't know how this happened. I look at you and I think, you've come out wrong, all of you. There's something not quite right about how you've turned out. Not what I expected.

MARY.   What a pity. After all your sterling efforts.

VI.   You seem like nice, personable people. I expect you are, but I don't know what you've got to do with me. You're closed off. I can't seem to get the hang of any of you. You don't tell me anything. I tell you things. What I did, where I went. And you just look irritated. You've no patience with me. No tolerance. And I had years of patience with you. It's not fair. How dare you? That's what I feel. How dare you?

MARY.   How dare I what?

VI.   Sometimes when I'm talking and I know you're not really listening, I could tear your heads from your bodies. I could tear you apart with my teeth. All of you. You behave as if I'd no hand in the making of you. I took you on picnics, I got up in the night for you. And you remember the things you didn't have. Holidays not gone on. Bicycles never got. A particular type of shoe. How was I to know? When are we going to be done with this? I hear you talking and I think your memories aren't the same as mine. I remember the time of your childhood, and it seems to me that you don't remember it because you weren't there —

MARY.   Why are you doing this to me? Why don't you do it to Teresa or Catherine?

VI.   How d'you know I don't? *(She strokes the clothes left on the bed.)* All my lovely dresses.

MARY.   I'm sorry. It's not as if you're going to be needing them. *(She begins to stuff them into black bags.)*

VI.   You were in my bed with him.

MARY.   He was cold. We didn't do anything.

VI.   You wanted to.

MARY.   Has nothing changed? You used to read my diaries, you knew about every boyfriend I ever had. You used to poke about my room. I always knew you were doing it, I used to watch you.

VI.   I had good reason.

MARY.   You did not. D'you understand? You did not. Ever. Nothing gave you the right to sift through my life like that.

VI.   What is it you don't have? What's the word? Humility, is that it? I've watched you being offered the world on a plate. And all of it you've taken, without a backwards glance. Lovers, sex. Exotic sex probably. Whatever that is. All tasted and discarded. You take it in your stride, these trips to Paris, these shoes from Milan, this bottle of wine and not that one, this man and not that one. This choosing and refusing —

MARY.   You know nothing —

VI.   I know different things. I know wanting and no choice. That counts too. It's not nothing. Excitement was a delivery of ornamental door-knockers. You drink champagne because you feel like it, you buy things with plastic cards. I've wanted that. I've tasted bile in my mouth with wanting it. And you carry it so lightly, you're not even grateful. I look at your easiness with the world and I don't know how I spawned you. But I started it. I taught you to speak properly, I saved you from your own stupid mistakes —

MARY.   It wasn't stupidity, it was ignorance, and for that I blame you —

VI.   I made sure you'd get somewhere, I made sure of it —

MARY.   Your idea of getting somewhere was marrying a dentist in a sheepskin coat from the Rotary Club —

VI.   You invent these versions of me and I don't recognize myself —

MARY.   I'm not listening to you —

VI.   I'm proud of you and you're ashamed of me —

MARY.   I am not —

VI.   I hear you say it all the time. I'm not like my mother, I'm not, I'm not. I'm like my father. Look in the mirror. Why can't you see it? Everyone else can. Look at the curve of your cheek, look at your hands, the way they move. You're doing it now. That's me. I got it from my mother. She got it from her mother. And on it goes, so far back that we don't know who began it or on what impulse, but we do it, we can't help it —

MARY. I've inherited some of your gestures. So what?

VI. Don't try and reinvent yourself with me. I know who you are.

MARY. You don't know anything.

VI. I look at you and I see myself.

MARY. Have you finished?

VI. Never. *(Go to black.)*

Scene 2

Same place. Catherine is praying to the telephone.

CATHERINE. Ring ring ring, please God, make him ring. Holy Mary Mother of God, I'll come back to the church, I'll do anything, make him ring now. Xavier, listen to me, pick up the fucking phone, please, I'm going off my head. I can't stand this. Why are you doing this to me? It's not fair. I'm getting an ulcer, you're making me ill. OK, I'm going to count to ten and then I'm going to phone you. If you haven't phoned by the time I've finished this joint I'm going to ring you, can you hear me? Just pick up the phone and speak to me. You could be dead for all I know, you could have had an accident or anything. Xavier, this is killing me. *(Mary comes in. Catherine looks at her.)* God, I hate him. *(She picks up the phone and taps out a number.)* Hola? Xavier, por favor ... Oh, right ... It's Catherine ... Catherine ... I just wondered if he got my message because I tried to leave a number but the line went dead ... Oh, I see ... When? ... Well, what time were you thinking he might ... OK, could you tell him then, just tell him that I called, and if he could — *(The line goes dead.)* Hello? Hello? *(Teresa and Frank come in as she puts the phone down.)*

TERESA.   Did he call then?

CATHERINE.   Yeah, yeah, he just rang, that was him — *(Mary turns to look at her. Catherine refuses to catch her eye.)*

TERESA.   Where's Mike?

MARY.   I've put him in a hot bath, he'd gone a bit blue.

TERESA.   Look we've got to sort these flowers out, just look at the photos, will you? It'll take two minutes — *(She hands the florist's book to Mary.)*

CATHERINE.   Poor thing, he hasn't had a chance to get to the phone, there's been a flood in the restaurant, all the furniture's bobbing around in three feet of water, it's a disaster, but it'll come off the insurance, I suppose. So that's all right. Luckily.

TERESA.   Oh dear. Frank, take those bags out to the car.

CATHERINE.   I just hope he can make the funeral, I mean I hope it's all sorted out so he can get a flight tonight, otherwise, well, he won't, will he? Make the funeral. *(Frank picks up an armful of black plastic.)*

FRANK.   Had he ever met your mother?

CATHERINE.   He'd talked to her on the phone. Anyway, what's that supposed to mean? God, why does everyone in this house have to be so oblique and sneery, why can't anyone say what they mean?

FRANK.   Catherine, stop being so bloody paranoid —

TERESA.   Frank. Bags. Car. Now. *(Frank pulls the bags down.)*

FRANK.   For Christ's sake, Teresa, I've only just thawed out.

CATHERINE.   Mike's never met her either and no one's complaining about him coming —

TERESA.   OK, OK, so what did he say?

CATHERINE.   Nothing. He said he'd phone back as soon as he knew what was happening. That's what he said. Stop interrogating me, OK?

MARY.   I'll have number seventeen B. *(She hands the book back to Teresa.)*

TERESA.   *(Looking at the photo.)* She was allergic to lilies of the valley, choose something else —

MARY. She's hardly going to start sneezing at her own funeral, is she? *(She takes the book again. Frank grapples with the bags, one of which bursts open.)*

FRANK. Oh, for fuck's sake! *(Mike comes in wrapped in a towel, clutching his clothes. He looks at the assembled crowd.)*

TERESA. Sorry Mike, d'you want to get dressed?

MIKE. No no, I'm fine really, don't mind me.

CATHERINE. I bet you've used all the water —

MARY. *(Handing the florist's book to Teresa.)* Twenty-seven A, not a lily in sight, absolutely no chance of impetigo, hives, or nervous eczema for either mourners or deceased. Catherine, you choose and then could you all leave us in peace for five minutes?

CATHERINE. Why are you always trying to get rid of me?

TERESA. Oh don't start, Catherine. Choose your wreath for heaven's sake — *(She tries to give her the book.)*

CATHERINE. No, I always get this, "Bugger off Catherine, we don't want you here," well, what am I supposed to do? Teresa's got Frank, you've got him, and what am I supposed to do on my own? I don't want to sit in the living room on my own while everyone else has smoochy secret conversations, it's not fair, not at a time like this, but if that's what you want — *(She gets into the wardrobe and shuts the door.)*

FRANK. Have you ever thought of laying off the drugs for a while, Catherine?

CATHERINE. Who asked you? *(The phone rings. She dives out of the wardrobe and grabs it.)* Hello? Xavier ... God, how are you, where've you been? Did you get my ... Oh, right ... Oh ... Right ... What? ... Oh. Well, couldn't you ... *(Long pause. She listens.)* I don't think we should ... maybe we should talk about this when I get back ... Oh ...OK, bye ... *(She puts the phone down. They all look at her. Awkward silence.)* He can't come.

TERESA. Because of the flood?

CATHERINE. The what? Oh, no, well, yes, lots of things. Anyway, he's not coming. *(Silence.)*

MIKE. Are you all right?

CATHERINE. Yeah. Yeah. He said he'd ring back later. *(She gets up.)* So. What is there still to do? Shall we sort the drawers out?

There's all the jewellery and stuff — *(She goes to the dressing table drawer and begins to rummage through it, taking things out haphazardly.)* God, he's so funny sometimes, he's so apologetic. He was almost crying on the phone, you should have heard him. It's just a real drag he can't come, he's so lovely. Did I ever show you his photo? He's got beautiful teeth. I mean, he really, really wanted to come. It's just hopeless, you know, running a restaurant and everything, you never get any time off.

MIKE. Maybe you'd like a cup of tea?

CATHERINE. I don't want any tea. *(She takes a tin from the drawer and tries to open it.)*

MIKE. Right. OK.

MARY. It's probably just as well he isn't coming. I mean, he wouldn't know anyone and it's a strange country and everything.

CATHERINE. Yes. It's probably just as well. *(She hurls the tin across the room, narrowly missing Frank.)*

FRANK. *(Ducking.)* Jesus —

CATHERINE. Fuck it! *(Silence. She bursts into racking sobs.)* I went to this counsellor — did I tell you this? — or a therapist or something and she said I had this problem and the problem was, I give too much, I just do too much for other people, I'm just a very giving person, and I never get any credit for any of it. I haven't even got any friends. I mean, I have but I don't like most of them, especially the women, and I try really hard, it's just I'm very sensitive and I get taken for a ride, nothing, ever goes right, every time, I mean, every time it's the same — like with men. What is it with men? I mean, I don't have a problem with men or anything. I love men. I've been to bed with seventy-eight of them, I counted, so obviously there's not a problem or anything, it's just he didn't even apologize or anything and how can he say on the phone he doesn't want to see me anymore? I mean, why now? Why couldn't he have waited? I don't know what to do, why does it always go wrong? I don't want to be on my own, I'm sick of people saying I'll be better off on my own, I'm not that sort of person, I can't do it. I did everything for him, I was patient and all the things you're supposed to be and people kept saying don't accept this from him, don't accept that, like, you know,

46

when he stayed out all night, not very often, I mean once or twice, and everyone said tell him to fuck off, but how could I because what if he did? Because they all do, everyone I've ever met does, they all disappear and I don't know if it's me or what. I don't want to be on my own, I can't stand it, I know it's supposed to be great but I don't think it is. I can't help it, it's no good pretending, it's fucking lonely and I can't bear it. *(She rushes out of the room. They look at each other. Silence. Frank picks up the tin.)*
FRANK.   She nearly had my head off.
MARY.   Christ. I wonder what sort of therapist she went to. How could anyone in their right mind tell Catherine her problem was give give give? *(She pours herself a whiskey.)*
MIKE.   Actually, it is, in a weird kind of way, she's trying to give you something all the time. It's usually inappropriate, that's all. I mean, she's obviously got some kind of problem.
TERESA.   Yes, we don't need you to tell us that, thank you —
MIKE.   Sorry, she's just, I mean, pretty miserable and not very stable —
TERESA.   Thank you, doctor —
FRANK.   Teresa —
TERESA.   Well, I'm sick or people feeling sorry for her. It's very easy the first time you meet her, but if you put up with her year in year out, you just want to kill her — *(She takes the glass from Mary.)* Give me some of that.
FRANK.   Teresa, don't drink whiskey, it makes you demented, you know that — *(Teresa knocks back the entire glass and grimaces.)*
TERESA.   Salt.
FRANK.   Don't drink it if it tastes of salt —
TERESA.   I thought you were taking those bags to the car —
MIKE.   Maybe one of you should go and have a word with Catherine.
TERESA.   How dare you walk in here and pontificate?
FRANK.   Put the bottle down, Teresa —
MIKE.   I just meant —
MARY.   Don't get involved, Mike, please.
MIKE.   I'm just saying from an outsider's point of view, she gets a rough deal. I know you can't see it, because your tolerance has

run out, but actually she's a mess and nobody really listens to
her —

TERESA.   Because she talks bollocks, that's why. I mean, this is
rich, this is, coming from you, the man who's been two-timing
his wife for the last five years telling us how to behave —

FRANK.   Teresa, what the hell's this got to do with anything?
Stop it.

TERESA.   No, why shouldn't I shout? Everyone else does in this
house —

FRANK.   I never said you were shouting —

TERESA.   Well, you're deaf then, because I am. Just answer me
this, Mike —

MARY.   Just ignore her —

TERESA.   When are you going to do the decent thing? When
are you going to leave your wife and marry my sister?

FRANK.   Oh, for Christ's sake, this is none of your business,
Teresa —

TERESA.   Well, it's about time someone asked —

FRANK.   But not you, and not now, OK?

MIKE.   It's very complicated.

MARY.   You don't have to answer, Mike, it's OK. Teresa, can we
stop this right here?

MIKE.   My wife's ill actually —

TERESA.   Oh, very convenient.

MARY.   She's got M.E.

TERESA.   M.E. my arse.

FRANK.   Teresa, I'm warning you —

TERESA.   What sort of illness is that?

MARY.   Stop it!

TERESA.   The sort of illness where you lie on the sofa for six
months with a bit of a headache. It's not a proper illness. It's not
a brain tumour. It's not as if she's got both her legs in traction.
Let me tell you something, Mike.

FRANK.   I don't think you should tell anybody anything right at
this moment —

TERESA.   There's nothing wrong with your wife, Mike.

MIKE. Well, there is actually.

TERESA. No. She knows you're having an affair so she thinks if she's ill, you won't leave her.

FRANK. Sorry about this, Mike, like you said, it's the grief, you know —

MIKE. Don't worry about it. I'm sorry, I shouldn't have stuck my oar in —

FRANK. Teresa, come on now, you're talking shite, come and have a lie down.

TERESA. Actually, I'm not talking shite. Actually, I've done it. I've got ill so people would be nice to me. I used to do it to my ex-husband. Sometimes it's all that's left to you. You get ill for a reason. You do it so people won't go.

FRANK. Teresa, I beg of you. Remember the last time. Three small gins, that's all. Took her bloody clothes off. In a car park.

TERESA. I was hot.

MARY. Give me the bottle. Now.

TERESA. Don't tell me what to do, and stop looking so bloody superior, because you've no cause —

MARY. His wife is ill. Genuinely ill. M.E. is real. It's not imaginary. OK?

TERESA. You see. We're our mother's daughters. Always take the man's side even when he's a complete pile of crap —

FRANK. Teresa, that's enough —

TERESA. Just like with Dad.

MARY. Frank, get her out of here —

TERESA. Our father, Mike, hardly spoke at all during the forty-eight years he was married to our mother. D'you remember hearing him speak, Mary? D'you recall him ever uttering a word of encouragement, an endearment?

MARY. Teresa —

TERESA. He was like a professional mute. And fucking someone else for most of the time.

FRANK. Right, that's it. Come on.

TERESA. D'you know what his last words were, Mike?

MIKE. I don't, no.

49

TERESA.   "Pass the mustard, Marjorie."

FRANK.   That was George the Fifth —

TERESA.   And she wasn't even called Marjorie. D'you understand?

MARY.   For Christ's sake, this is all bollocks.

TERESA.   Our mother's name was Violet and he said "Pass the mustard, Marjorie." I think that just about sums him up.

MARY.   This is pure invention —

TERESA.   How do you know? You weren't there. As usual. Never there in a crisis, not even your own. It's always someone else does the clearing up. Always me and Mum.

FRANK.   Teresa —

TERESA.   All those years she never said a word against him. Dad was always right, it was a perfect marriage. We've no secrets, she used to say. For heaven's sake. Who was she trying to kid?

MARY.   Teresa, please, I'm exhausted with this —

TERESA.   No! Who was she trying to kid? Tell me.

MARY.   I don't know. Herself. She was trying to kid herself. OK?

FRANK.   Mike, believe me, I'm on your side —

TERESA.   She dyed her hair red, d'you remember that? Dad didn't even notice. Didn't say a word. I mean you could hardly miss it, it was a disaster, dogs ran away from her in the street —

MARY.   He was being polite. He didn't want to hurt her —

TERESA.   Stop putting a gloss on him, he didn't bloody care. We could have had three heads and he'd not have noticed. Our entire bloody lives spent making sure nothing ruffled his feathers. He used to laugh at the word stress. "Stress," he'd say, "what a lot of rubbish." He said he didn't know what it was. Of course he bloody didn't. We did it for him. We contorted ourselves. Literally, in your case —

MARY.   I really don't want to get into this at the moment —

TERESA.   I don't believe he didn't know. How could he not bloody know? I mean, he might have been mute but he wasn't blind for goodness' sake —

MARY.   Yeah, well, it was a long time ago, let's just —

TERESA.   No, let's not, let's not just pretend it never happened —

50

MARY. Nothing happened —

TERESA. Bloody hell, how can you not notice that someone's eight months pregnant? *(Silence.)*

FRANK. Who was eight months pregnant? *(Silence.)*

MARY. Me. *(Pause.)*

TERESA. She was fourteen.

FRANK. Are you serious?

MARY. Yes. Anything else you'd like to know?

MIKE. You never told me —

MARY. It was a long time ago. There's nothing to tell —

TERESA. What d'you mean, there's nothing to tell?

MARY. It's for me to tell or not. If I don't talk about it, that's my business. It didn't happen to you, it happened to me.

TERESA. Oh typical sollipsistic bollocks. No one exists but you. Have you any idea what Mum and I went through?

MARY. You went through nothing. What you went through was nothing, d'you understand me? No, I don't suppose you do, you stupid, unimaginative woman.

FRANK. You're really excelling yourself today, Teresa. Although personally, I think your timing's a bit off. Much more effective if you'd waited till the funeral, and then got up and announced it to the congregation. You could have done it instead of the crappy Dylan Thomas poem. You'd have brought the house down.

TERESA. I'm tired of it. Why should she sail through her life getting pats on the back as if she'd never put a foot wrong?

FRANK. It just strikes me as being a strange time to reveal it to the world, Teresa. I mean, it hardly qualifies as bereavement counselling —

TERESA. You don't know the half of it — *(She picks up the bottle again.)*

FRANK. If you take one more swig of that, your liver will explode —

TERESA. Hiding it all from Dad. It was ridiculous, but of course Mary was Goody Two Shoes, Snow White and Our Lady of Lourdes all rolled into one as far as he was concerned, and we couldn't disabuse him of that convenient fiction, could we?

MARY. This is a novel told entirely from your point of view —

TERESA. Mum had to arrange everything, poor woman, all those lies about peritonitis and hospitals and God knows what —

MARY. She put her hand over my mouth when the pains started. I bet you've forgotten that bit —

TERESA. She did not. She found a lovely, Catholic family who brought him up in the true faith, while you got on with your true vocation of being the best at everything. No questions asked, never mention it again, it never happened, even Catherine doesn't know. Poor bloody Catherine, she's always complaining no one tells her anything, and she's right, no one ever did, no one ever will —

MIKE. So there's a grown-up son somewhere —

TERESA. Mary this, Mary that, Mary's bloody homework, Mary's bloody exams. We used to creep around on tiptoes in case her precious brain cells got thrown off-kilter by sudden exposure to pop music or someone slamming the front door. And all it's done is make her think she's immune, with her breathtaking fucking arrogance —

MARY. This is a fabrication, this is a complete distortion of the truth —

TERESA. And you still think you're unassailable, you still bloody do —

MARY. You're drunk, I'm not listening to this — (*She walks out furiously. Mike hurries after her.*)

MIKE. I'll just, er ... Excuse me a minute — Mary —

FRANK. D'you know something, Teresa, you're not just embarrassing, you're really quite repulsive, when you're drunk. I'm going to give Mike some friendly advice: Don't leave your wife. You don't want to marry into this lot. It's worse than the Borgias.

TERESA. Oh, shut up. (*She starts to cry. Long silence. Tears stream down her face.*) I've wanted to cry for three days. (*She takes another swig of whiskey, sobbing.*) The salt taste's gone. (*Silence.*) Say something, Frank. (*Pause.*)

FRANK. I've been awake for thirty-six hours. (*Pause.*)

TERESA. You have a whole repertoire of silences, don't you?

FRANK. Sorry?

TERESA. You've got a pissed-off one, and a resentful one, an I-hate-you-so-much-I'm-pretending-to-be-deaf one, and a worse one which is I-hate-you-so-much-I'm-pretending-to-be-foreign-and-I-don't-understand-anything-you're-saying. Your silences are the most eloquent thing about you. I can read them the way an Eskimo reads snow.

FRANK.   Inuit.

TERESA.   What?

FRANK.   Inuit. That's what they're called now. They don't like being called Eskimos any more.

TERESA.   How do you know? How many Eskimos have you ever met?

FRANK.   Teresa, I'm shattered —

TERESA.   You're always shattered.

FRANK.   What's that supposed to mean?

TERESA.   You come home, stare at the wall and pass out. You can fall asleep over a supermarket trolley, I've seen you, you can even do it with your eyes open so you look like you're awake —

FRANK.   It's because you keep sending me to these bloody conferences, sales junkets, glee clubs ... Fuck, I don't know what they are most of the time, half the time I don't even know where I am —

TERESA.   I do not send you —

FRANK.   Well, you bloody go. You spend a week living on goose fat and pickled cabbage in some emerging democracy. You try persuading people who haven't seen a banana for six months that what they need is royal fucking jelly. Then try it for six months of every year and see how you feel. You wouldn't even make it as far as the supermarket to fall asleep. You'd probably be dead.

TERESA.   It's not my fault if Albanians haven't got bananas, it's not my fault —

FRANK.   I never said that — *(Teresa is very, very drunk.)*

TERESA.   Why is it all my fault?

FRANK.   Teresa, what is it that you want from me? I can't do a thing right. What is it that I'm doing wrong? *(Silence)*

TERESA.   Why d'you do this to me?

FRANK.   Why do I do what?

TERESA.   Oh he's so nice, Frank, isn't he, he's so good-natured. Well actually, I want to say, the minute he walks through his own front door, he's not nice, not remotely, he stops speaking in sentences, he just grunts, he's not the charming Frank you all think he is, he might as well be a hologram, it's a bloody nightmare, Frank, you're just like — *(She stops. Pause.)*

FRANK.   Just like who?

TERESA.   No one. Nothing. *(She looks at him.)* You said you were witty and entertaining. That's what you said.

FRANK.   Oh, don't start all this again —

TERESA.   Witty and entertaining and five foot eleven. Hah!

FRANK.   You said you were twenty-nine.

TERESA.   I did not say I was twenty-nine —

FRANK.   Excuse me, oh, excuse me — *(He takes a piece of paper from his wallet and reads.)* Thoughtful, sexy, vegetarian woman, coming up thirty —

TERESA.   — seeks witty, entertaining man thirty to forty-five —

FRANK.   You weren't coming up thirty —

TERESA.   And you weren't witty and entertaining.

FRANK.   You didn't argue at the time.

TERESA.   Say something entertaining, then. Go on.

FRANK.   Oh, for fuck's sake —

TERESA.   Well say something interesting, then. Tell me something new. *(Pause.)*

FRANK.   I hated *Hannah and Her Sisters*.

TERESA.   What?

FRANK.   I hated it. I hate Woody Allen.

TERESA.   *Hannah and Her Sisters* was our first date.

FRANK.   I know.

TERESA.   You said you loved it.

FRANK.   I was lying. I didn't get it. It wasn't funny.

TERESA.   There's that bit where the man won't buy the paintings because they don't match his sofa. That's funny.

FRANK.   It's not. It's perfectly reasonable. You wouldn't buy, say, a big green and purple painting if you had a red sofa, would you? You'd scream every time you went into the living room. You'd get migraine.

TERESA.   That's not the point of the joke.

FRANK.   So what is the point, then?

TERESA.   You've been pretending to like Woody Allen all these years. You've been lying. I've been married to a stranger — (*Pause. She looks at him unsteadily.*) Frank.

FRANK.   What?

TERESA.   Are you having an affair?

FRANK.   What?

TERESA.   Just tell me. (*Frank is bewildered.*)

FRANK.   I'm not having an affair.

TERESA.   Are you sure?

FRANK.   Oh hang on, let me rack my brains, it might have slipped my mind —

TERESA.   I'm serious —

FRANK.   I'm not having an affair. I haven't got the energy —

TERESA.   But if you ever. I mean. If you ever did have an affair you'd tell me, wouldn't you?

FRANK.   I thought that was the whole point of having an affair. You don't tell. (*Teresa punches him in the stomach. He gasps.*) I was joking. I was joking.

TERESA.   You've got a horrible sense of humour.

FRANK.   I'm sorry. Put the bottle down. Come on, you've had enough. Sit down. (*She hands him the bottle, tearfully. Pause. Frank takes a deep breath.*) Teresa. During the course of my spectacularly indirect journey here from Dusseldorf, in between bouts with the mime artist, I did a bit of thinking. Two and a half days at a health food convention being harassed by people who do vitamin therapy according to star signs reminded me of what deep down I've known for some time. We sell utter crap.

TERESA.   Frank —

FRANK.   No, hang on, let me finish. I know you believe in it. I know you do. But just answer this. Were your parents happy running a hardware shop? Running a business together?

TERESA.   No, of course not.

FRANK.   So why did you think you would be?

TERESA.   It's got nothing to do with my parents. (*Frank looks at her.*)

FRANK.   Maybe later, when the funeral's out of the way, we could, you know ...

TERESA.   What?

FRANK. I don't know. Maybe you should run the business and I should go into something else.

TERESA. Like what?

FRANK. The thing is Teresa, I hate selling things. Or specifically, I hate selling things that people don't want and I don't believe in. I'm not cut out for it. I like a nice straightforward transaction, you know? "Good evening, two pints of bitter, and a rum and coke." "Certainly sir, ice and lemon? That'll be five pounds fifty, thank you." End of transaction. Not, "Can I interest you in a double port while we're at it? No? Well what about a set of toning tables, or cavity wall insulation?" I can't stand it, Teresa, it's driving me insane. I want to do something simple.

TERESA. Such as what? *(Pause.)*

FRANK. A pub. I want to run a pub.

TERESA. You want to run a pub?

FRANK. I've seen one for sale just outside Ripon. *(Teresa staggers to her feet.)*

TERESA. A pub! I don't believe you — *(Catherine walks in.)*

CATHERINE. What's going on?

FRANK. Nothing's going on, I'm trying to have a conversation with Teresa —

TERESA. I think I'm going to be sick. No, don't come near me. A pub, you must be out of your mind —

FRANK. Teresa —

TERESA. Don't touch me. A pub, a pub for God's sake — *(She goes out. Crashing noises from outside the room. Swearing. Frank lies back on the bed, exhausted.)*

CATHERINE. Oh God. *(She jumps on to the bed next to Frank.)* I'm so depressed.

FRANK. Yeah, well, you know, it's a depressing business. Dying and what not. *(Silence.)*

CATHERINE. Frank?

FRANK. What?

CATHERINE. Am I unattractive?

FRANK. I'm sorry?

CATHERINE. D'you think I'm pretty?

FRANK. Of course you're pretty. Look Catherine, I'm exhausted, I'm talked out, I'm sorry. *(Pause.)*

CATHERINE. I'm very pretty. I'm good fun. I'm a very special person. That's what Carmen, my therapist, said. I'm a brilliant cook. So why did he leave me?

FRANK. Jesus, Catherine, I don't know. People leave each other. You'll get over it. I have to go and talk to Teresa.

CATHERINE. She's probably being sick. That's what she usually does if she drinks. What am I going to do?

FRANK. About what?

CATHERINE. Xavier.

FRANK. Catherine, I've no advice to give you. I'm a middle-aged man with a health food business I don't believe in, and a normally teetotal wife who's taken to the bottle. I could say, have some ginseng tea, ear organic vegetables and learn to love yourself, but it's all a lot of bollocks.

CATHERINE. I have to get back to him, I can't bear it. I have to see him, I mean, this is the real thing, I know it is, so I can't just give in can I? ... I can't bear it — (*She puts her head in his lap. He looks at her as if she's an unexploded bomb. He tries to move away. She puts her arms round him.*)

FRANK. OK, OK, OK, that's enough, Catherine, take it easy —

CATHERINE. I need a hug. (*He pats her awkwardly.*)

FRANK. There you go.

CATHERINE. That's not a hug.

FRANK. Teresa'll give you a hug.

CATHERINE. How can she, with her head down the toilet? (*She grips him tightly.*)

FRANK. Catherine, get off my leg —

CATHERINE. It's OK, you're family —

FRANK. Exactly —

CATHERINE. Hold me, Frank, I'm so bloody lonely. What am I going to do? I just need a bit of a hug, that's all —

FRANK. Catherine, I'm very flattered but steady on, eh, we don't want to — (*She kisses him, immediately pulls away and jumps off the bed.*)

CATHERINE. I wasn't trying to seduce you or anything.

FRANK. Catherine, you're a bit crazy at the moment, OK —

CATHERINE. Oh, typical —

FRANK. No, I mean, it's understandable, look at Teresa. If I were you I'd phone this Pepe now, and tell him to eff off, just say "I'm sorry, Pepe, my mother's just died, I don't need this, take a hike — "

CATHERINE. He's not called Pepe —

FRANK. Or whatever, Jose —

CATHERINE. Oh, for fuck's sake, all I wanted was a bit of affection. A bit of support. That's all I was asking for. I wasn't asking you to marry me and bear my children. What is it with men? Why d'you always have to misread this signals? God, you make me sick — *(Mary and Mike come in. Mary is carrying a tin box.)*

MARY. I know you're drawn to this room like moths to a flame, but believe me, I've had enough of all of you. If anyone rings I'll let you know —

CATHERINE. I was going anyway — *(She goes out. Frank gets up.)*

FRANK. I'm worried about her. I'm serious — she needs six months in a secure unit, she's completely — anyway, I'd better go and sort Teresa out — *(He goes. Mary sits on the bed and opens the box. She sifts through papers.)*

MARY. I'm putting my name on a register, so that if he's looking for me, he'll find me. I don't even know what he looks like. I have to make him up. I sit on tubes looking at twenty-five-year-old boys, and I think, maybe that's him. Ever since he went I've been looking for him, but he's like ether, I can't get hold of him. *(She unfolds a piece of paper.)* Oh, thank God. Thank God it's still here. Here he is. Oh, look. Patrick. Patrick James. My boy. I wanted to call him Heathcliff. I was fourteen. I still thought life was a novel. *(She reads.)* "Sex: boy. Name: Patrick James. Weight: six pounds four ounces." This is all I've got left of him. *(She looks round the room.)* This will all be gone soon. All this furniture, all this stuff. The room will go probably. It'll disappear into the sea. And this is all I want to take from the house. This is the only thing I want to salvage. So I can prove he's mine. *(She puts the paper in her bag. Puts her hand on her stomach, and goes to the mirror. Looks at herself sideways.)* It's a strange feeling being pregnant. You wake up one morning and you feel so absolutely other. *(She looks at him.)*

MIKE. Mary, I think, you know, you're jumping the gun here —

MARY. I need a real child, not a ghost one. What are you going to do? Are you sticking with me or walking away?

MIKE. If you are pregnant, *if* you are, of course, I mean of course I won't walk away, I just don't think it's — look, I know Charlie Morgan's in the Betty Ford clinic —

MARY. You could always sue him. Everyone else is.

MIKE. Look. I know you want a child, I accept that. I know you're furious with me for having a vasectomy —

MARY. Five years and you never mentioned it, that's what I can't —

MIKE. I don't want a child, Mary! I don't want a child. I can't want one just because you do. Love and paternity aren't indivisible in my mind. When I say I love you it means I like you, I want to be with you, I want to go to bed with you, it means all sorts of things but it doesn't necessarily mean three children and Sainsbury's every Saturday for the next thirty years —

MARY. No, you've already got that —

MIKE. I can't help what happened before I met you! You might not like what I'm telling you, but I can't lie to make you feel better. I never wanted kids in the first place. They happened and now I love them but I don't want any more. It's not because I'm cold or selfish — at least no more than anyone else is — it's that I feel sucked dry by what people need from me — patients, Chrissie, the children. You're where I come to be equal, I come to you because you're not asking to be healed. Some people aren't paternal. It's not a crime, I'm one of them. If you're a woman and you take care of your own fertility, nobody argues. Well, I've taken care of mine. I didn't have a vasectomy because Chrissie's ill, I had it for me. *(Silence.)* But obviously, you know, if you *are* pregnant. I'll stick by you.

MARY. Well, hey. That makes me feel a whole lot better. *(Pause.)* Jesus. Oh, Jesus, what a mess. Bring back the days when we had no choice in the matter.

MIKE. Well you did have a choice. You chose me.

MARY. O choice shmoice. Have you seen what's on offer out there? Tiny little trainspotters in grey shoes, maniacs, alcoholics, men who wear their underpants for a week. *(There's a knock at the door.)* Go away. *(Catherine comes in.)*

CATHERINE.   D'you know what she's gone and done?

MARY.   I don't know and I don't care.

CATHERINE.   I'll kill her — *(Frank comes in.)*

FRANK.   Look, I'm sorry, I know you're trying to get a bit of peace —

MARY.   Oh don't mind about us, please —

FRANK.   The thing is, Teresa's arranged for your mother to come back, that's all. *(Pause.)*

MARY.   Sorry, I'm obviously in the grip of an aural hallucination. Say that again.

CATHERINE.   The night before. She's coming back here. The night before the funeral. Tonight.

MARY.   What, in her coffin?

CATHERINE.   No she's coming on foot, what d'you think?

MARY.   Apart from anything else, where are we going to put her?

FRANK.   In here, this is her room.

MARY.   I'm sleeping in here. I can't sleep next to my dead mother. For Christ's sake.

MIKE.   We can go to a hotel —

FRANK.   You can have it open or closed, it's up to you.

CATHERINE.   She's dead. I don't want to see her dead face. *(Teresa appears in the doorway, drunk and dishevelled.)*

TERESA.   You should see her, it's important, and then you'll know she's dead —

CATHERINE.   She's been in a fridge for four days, of course she's bloody dead —

TERESA.   Well, I'm sorry, she's coming home, I've arranged it and that's that and it's no good saying why didn't I ask you because you weren't here to ask. She's coming home to spend her last night in her own bedroom. And that's the end of the story. The end. Full stop. *Finito. La fin. (She sways precariously.)* Frank ...

FRANK.   What?

TERESA.   I've had far too much to drink ... *(Go to black.)*

60

Scene 3

Same room, early next morning. The coffin is there on a low trestle. Teresa is dressed for the funeral, talking on the phone. Catherine is sitting in her dressing gown, staring at the coffin.

TERESA. So when you say "even later," you mean what? ... I see ... No, of course, I understand ... Could you ring as soon as — thank you ... Bye ... *(She looks at Catherine, looks at her watch.)* They must be snowed in.

CATHERINE. Who?

TERESA. The men who carry the coffin. Funeral operatives, he calls them. They still haven't shown up for work. He's trying to find some replacements. I wish I knew what he meant, I mean we don't want amateurs doing it. It's supposed to be dignified. You can't just get anyone in. *(Catherine says nothing. She's staring at the coffin.)* Why don't you get dressed, or are you thinking of going like that?

CATHERINE. It's tiny, isn't it? *(Teresa looks.)*

TERESA. She was only small.

CATHERINE. Not as small as that.

TERESA. She must have been. They don't fold them up. *(Pause.)*

CATHERINE. D'you think they make them to measure?

TERESA. I suppose they must.

CATHERINE. I suppose so. Yeah. I mean babies' coffins are tiny, aren't they? They're about this big.

TERESA. They'd have to be. Otherwise they'd rattle around.

CATHERINE. Mmmm ... Unless you used loads of bubble wrap.

TERESA. If you want to look at her, you just have to undo a little screw at the top. They gave me a wee screwdriver. *(Silence.)* I don't want to, do you?

CATHERINE. Not really, no. *(Pause. She turns away from the coffin.)* I'm so depressed. I can't change my flight.

TERESA. Forget him. He's a bastard.

CATHERINE. How do you know?

TERESA. You've never had a boyfriend who isn't. You don't go about it the right way.

CATHERINE. There was that nice Swiss one. He was all right. Did you ever meet him? He was gorgeous, I felt just like Heidi.

TERESA. I knew Frank was the right man for me straightaway. Because I chose him. I got forty-seven replies. I whittled them down and chose the most compatible.

CATHERINE. Yeah, but the thing is ...

TERESA. What?

CATHERINE. At the end of the day you still landed up with Frank.

TERESA. We're very, very happy actually. We're a perfect match. Because we went about it in the right way —

CATHERINE. D'you know who he reminds me of?

TERESA. Don't say it.

CATHERINE. He does though, doesn't he? It must be a bit depressing. You go through all the palaver of whittling out the dross and you end up married to your dad. *(Mary comes in, dressed for the funeral. She looks white and drawn.)*

TERESA. Oh, there you are. You look lovely. *(Pause. Mary looks at the coffin.)* How was the hotel?

MARY. Fine. *(Teresa watches her looking at the coffin.)* Sorry. It's a bit of a shock. Brings you up a bit short, doesn't it —

CATHERINE. Everyone's snowed in. There's no one to carry it —

TERESA. That's no reason to still be in your dressing gown —

CATHERINE. OK, OK, I'll get dressed, I'm going, don't worry. *(She goes out. Mary looks round the room, obviously searching for something.)*

TERESA. I'm sorry about yesterday.

MARY. Forget it.

TERESA. I shouldn't drink.

MARY. No. You shouldn't. *(She sits on the bed and takes the green tin from underneath. Begins to look through it. Teresa looks at her sharply.)*

TERESA. Where did you find that?

MARY. At the back of the airing cupboard. Why?

TERESA. When?

MARY. Yesterday. I wanted the copy of his birth certificate. *(Teresa snatches the tin from her.)*

TERESA. It's not in here. *(Mary is bewildered.)*

MARY. I know it's not. I took it out. I was just wondering if there was anything else —

TERESA. Like what?

MARY. I've no idea, adoption papers. For goodness' sake, what's the matter with you?

TERESA. It's just old gas bills and bus tickets, you know what she was like, she could never throw anything away —

MARY. I just want to see if there's anything else about Patrick —

TERESA. There's not, I've looked.

MARY. Teresa, this is ridiculous, I'm not in the mood, give me the tin. *(Teresa holds on to it grimly, unable to think of a response.)* Please.

TERESA. I'll give it to you later. After the funeral. OK?

MARY. Why can't I have it now?

TERESA. We'll sort it out later, OK.

MARY. Sort what out? Give me the tin, for goodness' sake — *(She makes a grab for it. A tussle.)*

TERESA. I told you, I'll give it to you later — *(More tussling.)*

MARY. What is it?

TERESA. Nothing! *(Tussle gets more violent.)*

MARY. Give me the bloody tin! *(They fight. Teresa manages to hang on. She sits down with the tin.)* Teresa, what the fuck is this about?!

TERESA. Nothing. Nothing. I'll tell you later —

MARY. Tell me now.

TERESA. I can't. *(Pause.)*

MARY. It's about Patrick, isn't it? *(Teresa looks stricken. Pause.)*

TERESA. There're some cuttings in here about him. Newspaper cuttings.

MARY. You know where he is? *(Pause.)* Where is he? *(Pause.)*

TERESA. He's dead. *(Silence.)* I'm sorry. I wanted to tell you. I would have. I would have. I'm sorry. I told Mum, but she said no, and then ... I mean, and then it was ... I mean, the moment had passed — *(Silence.)*

MARY. What happened to him?

TERESA. Some cliffs gave way. Just outside Whitby. Him and another boy. Father Michael told us.

FRANK. *(Off.)* Teresa! What's happened to my trousers?

TERESA. I meant to tell you, but when? When could we have told you?

MARY. When it happened. Why didn't you tell me when it happened?

TERESA. *(Offering her the tin, gently.)* They're in an envelope marked medical cards. The cuttings.

FRANK. *(Off.)* Teresa!

MARY. Go to him. Don't let him come in here.

TERESA. Mary, I'm sorry —

MARY. Go. *(She goes. The lighting changes to the bluish-green glow. Faint sound of big band music in the distance. Vi appears in the open doorway. Her hair is now completely white. She looks at the coffin.)*

VI. Open the box. *(She goes over to the coffin. Mary says nothing.)* It's open. Look. *(She lifts the top section of the lid and looks.)* A bloody old woman. I don't recognize her. A bloody old woman in green eyeshadow. Green. They call this dignity, apparently. Green frosted eyeshadow. *(She shuts the lid. Closes her eyes and sways gently to the music.)* I just want one last dance before I go ... *(Mary watches her for a while. Empties the stuff out of the tin. Finds the envelope, takes out cuttings. Looks at them in bewilderment.)*

MARY. Nineteen eighty ... Nineteen eighty ... Why didn't you tell me? *(Vi stops dancing. Pause.)*

VI. It seemed right at the time. You were doing your finals. *(Silence.)*

MARY. I've been waiting for him all these years. I've been waiting for him to turn up and claim me.

VI. Don't become one of those women who blame. Don't be a victim. It's beneath you.

MARY. You made me give him away because it was embarrassing.

VI. I wanted you to do well. I didn't want you to be trapped. I did it for you.

MARY. I look at this patient of mine. This twenty-year-old boy lying in a hospital bed, completely blank, no memory of anything at all, just an empty vessel. And all I see is Patrick. Full of memories that I didn't put there, that someone else filled him with. And I think, did I give him anything? Is there some part of him that's still mine? Maybe he smiles like me. Maybe he walks like me. Maybe he doesn't. You made me obsessed.

VI. I thought nothing could shake you. I was wrong. *(Pause.)*

MARY. Last night, I dreamt I was in a fishmonger's. On the slab, there was a box. It seemed to be full of chickens. Trussed. I couldn't be sure. "Are they chickens?" I said. He pulled back the sacking and they weren't chickens but babies. Dead trussed babies, no bigger than my hand. When I woke up, blood. I'm not pregnant. I never was. Everything's dead. I can't bear it. I can't hold on to anything.

VI. Despair is the last refuge of the ego. *(Pause.)* I got that out of *Reader's Digest*. *(Pause.)*

MARY. I'm in a freefall. I opened a door and stepped out into thin air.

VI. I never knew how you felt. I never know how you felt about anything. You thought your feelings were too rarefied to share with me. You count me out. You looked straight through me. You shared nothing with me, not a joke, not a smile that wasn't patronizing, you never let me in, you never let me know you. This stony punishment all these years, wanting me to be better than I am, always your mother, always responsible, always to blame. How could I apologize, when you wouldn't give me room? *(Silence.)*

MARY. I'm sorry. *(Pause.)* What was it like? The last few months?

VI. It's been a long time since you asked me a proper question. It's been a long time since you allowed me to know more than you.

MARY. Tell me what it felt like.

VI. Like I had holes in my brain. Frightening. Huge rips. I'd not recognize people. You just think, where am I? What's going on? And then you don't know what you mean when you say "I". It doesn't seem to mean anything.

MARY. You always still looked like you. Like essence of you. The way you moved your hands sometimes. Your laugh.

VI. Some things stay. Some things are in your bones. Songs. Babies. I was very keen on babies. Dogs. People's hair. Dancing. I wanted to dance. Usually in what Teresa called inappropriate places. Like the garden.

MARY. But who did you feel like? Who are you if you take your memory away?

VI. I felt like I'd gone away. Like I'd broken up into islands and in between was just a terrible muddle of old songs and odd names drifting by, men I vaguely recognized. I felt like a cut-up thing. But sometimes the pieces would float to the surface, drift back together, and there I was, washed ashore from a pitch black sea of nothing. Me. Still me. I'm still here. *(Pause.)* Forgiving someone's just like throwing a switch.

MARY. Is it?

VI. It's just a decision. And afterwards you're free. *(Pause.)* I've done it.

MARY. Have you?

VI. I forgave your father. And now I'll forgive you. But it's time I went. *(She goes to the mirror and looks at herself.)* Yes. I think it is.

MARY. Mum. Don't go just yet — *(Vi gives her one last look before she goes. Mary puts her head in her hands and cries. Teresa and Frank come in.)*

TERESA. Frank, get the Rescue Remedy.

FRANK. She needs a bloody drink. *(She takes hold of her.)*

TERESA. Mary, pull yourself together, you've got a funeral to go to. Frank, she needs Rescue Remedy, now — *(Frank goes out.)*

MARY. I'm past rescuing —

TERESA. Take some of these — *(She tries to give her some tablets.)*

MARY. What are they?

TERESA. Aconite, it's just a matter of —

MARY. It's not just a matter of anything, it's my life! Stop trying to make it little and solvable, stop trying to sort it out with vitamin pills!

TERESA. They're not vitamin pills —

MARY. There's no cure. *(Frank comes in with Mike. Mike goes to her.)*

66

FRANK. Rescue Remedy. Duty-free Vodka. Take your pick.

MIKE. Are you all right?

MARY. I'm tired, I didn't sleep.

FRANK. I read somewhere the other day that if you eat a whole lettuce before you go to bed, it has pretty much the same effect as a Mogadon.

MARY. Well I'm torn now. I don't know whether to have a Caesar salad or cut my throat. *(She takes the Rescue Remedy from Frank, and downs the lot.)*

TERESA. No, no, you just need a few drops —

MARY. There you are, I feel better already. Suddenly life makes sense, suddenly my mother's not dead, I am actually pregnant, in fact it's triplets. Suddenly there is meaning where there was none before. Suddenly I'm Princess Michael of fucking Kent. *(She sits sown, exhausted. Silence.)*

TERESA. Pregnant?

MARY. A fantasy.

MIKE. Sorry?

MARY. I thought I was pregnant, but I'm not. It was a phantom. You obviously caught Charlie Morgan on a good day.

TERESA. *(Desperately.)* Oh, why don't you two have a baby? Why don't you? Leave your wife and have a baby with Mary — *(The door opens and Catherine appears, in a very short skirt.)*

CATHERINE. Hi. What d'you think? *(They look at her in confusion.)*

TERESA. What?

CATHERINE. The outfit. What d'you think?

FRANK. Sorry?

CATHERINE. Do I look all right? *(Silence.)*

FRANK. Very nice.

TERESA. It's half-way up your bottom.

CATHERINE. It's the only one I've got. Mary, d'you like it?

MARY. Apart from the fact that you can see your ovaries, it's fine — *(The phone rings and Frank picks it up.)*

FRANK. Hello? ... Oh, Jesus wept ... And what? You've got what? ... I don't believe this ... Can we what? I beg your pardon? ... I'm sorry? Well, I mean, I suppose if ... Right, OK, OK, thanks, OK. *(He puts the phone down.)* He's on his way. He says, do we have any gentleman who can give him a hand? Taking the coffin out to the hearse. *(Pause.)*

MIKE. Fine, right, OK, no problem, absolutely.

FRANK. I think he said it's a bit difficult for him because he's got a *plastic hand.* Is my hearing going or what?

TERESA. I'm afraid not, no. *(Catherine is staring at the coffin.)*

CATHERINE. Did you open the lid?

TERESA. No.

CATHERINE. It's so weird.

TERESA. What is?

CATHERINE. It's weird she's in this box. I mean, I can't imagine it.

FRANK. I don't think you're supposed to.

TERESA. You can't help it though, can you? Actually, if you think about it, it could be anyone in here. We'd never know the difference.

CATHERINE. We'll never see her again. And she's so close. She had such a nice face. *(Pause.)* I wish she wasn't dead.

MIKE. Maybe we could all do with a drink. *(He begins to pour whiskey for everyone. Teresa puts her arm round Catherine.)*

CATHERINE. I'm all right. I'll be OK. I'll be OK. I will. *(Mike hands out drinks. Awkward silence.)*

FRANK. Whoops. Nearly said cheers. *(Silence.)* So. Here we are then. *(He looks at his watch. Then at the coffin.)* I presume it's a veneer, is it?

TERESA. What?

FRANK. The coffin. Chipboard and veneer. *(They all look at the coffin.)*

MARY. Well, you know, we were going for the jewel-encrusted mother of pearl but we thought this would burn better. *(Silence.)* Sorry.

FRANK. You can get do-it-yourself coffins now, apparently. Made of cardboard.

MARY. Oh, good.

MIKE. Something to do in the long winter evenings. Build your own coffin. *(Sound of a car horn from outside. Mary goes to the window.)*

68

MARY. That'll be him.

MIKE. Right. OK. Shall we, er ... Frank?

FRANK. God. Right. I'll take this end, shall I? *(He takes one end of the coffin.)*

MIKE. Keep your back straight — *(They lift.)*

FRANK. I'll go backwards, or would you rather?

MIKE. No, no, I'm fine — can someone hold the door? *(Teresa does so. They manoeuvre the coffin. Catherine starts to laugh madly.)*

CATHERINE. Poor Mum. Even her funeral's a cock-up.

MIKE. Pull her round to the right a bit — the right —

FRANK. Mind that bit of carpet — whoops, nearly ... that's it ... *(They go out. Off.)* To me, to me — *(The women pull on coats and gloves, etc.)*

MARY. Just check your phone's not in your bag will you?

TERESA. I've checked.

CATHERINE. I look ridiculous, don't I?

MARY. You don't. You look fine.

CATHERINE. I didn't hate her really.

MARY. I know that. We all know that. She didn't hate you either. *(Pause.)*

CATHERINE. D'you remember, when Dad was out sometimes, she used to get us up in the middle of the night and give us crisps and ice cream soda?

MARY. And she'd have a Dubonnet and lemonade. God, I'd forgotten about that.

TERESA. She called it a girls' night in.

CATHERINE. We were all sleepy in our pajamas, and she'd put on Nat King Cole. *(Pause.)*

MARY. She must have been lonely. I never thought of that. *(Silence.)*

CATHERINE. I put a hip flask in my bag in case we need it.

TERESA. I think I'll pass on that, if you don't mind.

MARY. Got tissues?

TERESA. Yes. *(Frank and Mike come in.)*

FRANK. Are we set?

TERESA. I think so. Shall we go, then? Are we ready?

MARY. You go on ahead. I'll be out in a minute

TERESA.   Come with us, Catherine. Come on. *(Frank, Teresa and Catherine go out. Teresa with her arm around Catherine. Silence. Mary and Mike look at each other.)*

MARY.   I think maybe that French guy was right.

MIKE.   Sorry?

MARY.   The one who said water was like magnetic tape. My mother's the ghost in the machine. She goes through us like wine through water. Whether we like it or not. Nothing ends entirely.

MIKE.   What are you going to do?

MARY.   Can you live a rich life without a child?

MIKE.   You know you can. *(Pause.)*

MARY.   Yes. I suppose so. *(Pause.)* I'm going to ask you something, Mike. I'm going to ask it once and I'll never ask it again. Leave your wife and come with me. *(Pause.)*

MIKE.   I think ... I don't think we should talk about this now. Maybe we should talk about it after the funeral ...

MARY.   I'm not asking you to talk about it. Take your chance, Mike. *(Pause.)*

MIKE.   *(Almost a whisper.)* Maybe afterwards we could ... *(She goes to the window. He looks at her helplessly. She looks out of the window.)*

MARY.   This snow's never going to stop. Everything frozen in its tracks. Everything cancelled.

TERESA.   *(Off.)* Mary!

MARY.   I've hated winter all my life. Ice on the windows, dark at three in the afternoon. Sea fret freezing the hairs in your nostrils. I've hated the stasis, the waiting for spring.

TERESA.   *(Off.)* Mary! *(She turns to Mike.)*

MIKE.   What are you going to do?

MARY.   Learn to love the cold. *(They go out. As they leave, the lights dim to gold and blue. The curtains billow in the room and a flurry of snow drifts in. Nat King Cole* plays faintly in the distance. Fade down lights.)*

CURTAIN

---

*See Special Note on Songs and Recordings on copyright page.

70

PROPERTY LIST

Clutchbag (VI) with:
  cigarettes and lighter
Books (VI, TERESA)
Portable alarm clock (MARY)
Breast pump (MARY)
Whiskey bottle (MARY)
Carrier bags (CATHERINE) with:
  clothing
Bottle of paracetamol (CATHERINE)
Bag (TERESA)
Bottle of pills (TERESA)
Joints (CATHERINE)
Electronic organizer (TERESA)
Florist's book of photographs (TERESA)
Bread knife (CATHERINE)
Sandwich (CATHERINE)
Glass (CATHERINE)
Black bin liners (TERESA)
Suitcase (FRANK)
Camera (CATHERINE)
Tin (CATHERINE)
Green tin box (MARY) with:
  papers
  envelopes with newspaper cuttings
Drinks (MIKE)
Coffin
Various articles in wardrobe (throughout):
  dresses
  hats
  frocks
  shoes
  lipstick
  earrings

SOUND EFFECTS

Phone
Banging noise
Crashing noises
Big band music
Car horn

NEW PLAYS

• SMASH by Jeffrey Hatcher. Based on the novel, AN UNSOCIAL SOCIALIST by George Bernard Shaw, the story centers on a millionaire Socialist who leaves his bride on their wedding day because he fears his passion for her will get in the way of his plans to overthrow the British government. *"SMASH is witty, cunning, intelligent, and skillful."* –Seattle Weekly. *"SMASH is a wonderfully high-style British comedy of manners that evokes the world of Shaw's high-minded heroes and heroines, but shaped by a post modern sensibility."* –Seattle Herald. [5M, 5W] ISBN: 0-8222-1553-5

• PRIVATE EYES by Steven Dietz. A comedy of suspicion in which nothing is ever quite what it seems. *"Steven Dietz's ... Pirandellian smooch to the mercurial nature of theatrical illusion and romantic truth, Dietz's spiraling structure and breathless pacing provide enough of an oxygen rush to revive any moribund audience member ... Dietz's mastery of playmaking ... is cause for kudos."* –The Village Voice. *"The cleverest and most artful piece presented at the 21st annual [Humana] festival was PRIVATE EYES by writer-director Steven Dietz."* –The Chicago Tribune. [3M, 2W] ISBN: 0-8222-1619-1

• DIMLY PERCEIVED THREATS TO THE SYSTEM by Jon Klein. Reality and fantasy overlap with hilarious results as this unforgettable family attempts to survive the nineties. *"Here's a play whose point about fractured families goes to the heart, mind -- and ears."* –The Washington Post. *" ... an end-of-the millennium comedy about a family on the verge of a nervous breakdown ... Trenchant and hilarious ... "* –The Baltimore Sun. [2M, 4W] ISBN: 0-8222-1677-9

• HONOUR by Joanna Murray-Smith. In a series of intense confrontations, a wife, husband, lover and daughter negotiate the forces of passion, lust, history, responsibility and honour. *"Tight, crackling dialogue (usually played out in punchy verbal duels) captures characters unable to deal with emotions ... Murray-Smith effectively places her characters in situations that strip away pretense."* –Variety. *"HONOUR might just capture a few honors of its own."* –Time Out Magazine. [1M, 3W] ISBN: 0-8222-1683-3

• NINE ARMENIANS by Leslie Ayvazian. A revealing portrait of three generations of an Armenian-American family. *" ... Ayvazian's obvious personal exploration ... is evocative, and her picture of an American Life colored nostalgically by an increasingly alien ethnic tradition, is persuasively embedded into a script of a certain supple grace ... "* –The NY Post. *"... NINE ARMENIANS is a warm, likable work that benefits from ... Ayvazian's clear-headed insight into the dynamics of a close-knit family ... "* –Variety. [5M, 5W] ISBN: 0-8222-1602-7

• PSYCHOPATHIA SEXUALIS by John Patrick Shanley. Fetishes and psychiatry abound in this scathing comedy about a man and his father's argyle socks. *"John Patrick Shanley's new play, PSYCHOPATHIA SEXUALIS is ... perfectly poised between daffy comedy and believable human neurosis which Shanley combines so well ... "* –The LA Times. *"John Patrick Shanley's PSYCHOPATHIA SEXUALIS is a salty boulevard comedy with a bittersweet theme ... "* –New York Magazine. *"A tour de force of witty, barbed dialogue."* –Variety. [3M, 2W] ISBN: 0-8222-1615-9

DRAMATISTS PLAY SERVICE, INC.
440 Park Avenue South, New York, NY 10016 212-683-8960 Fax 212-213-1539
postmaster@dramatists.com www.dramatists.com

NEW PLAYS

• **A QUESTION OF MERCY by David Rabe.** The Obie Award-winning playwright probes the sensitive and controversial issue of doctor-assisted suicide in the age of AIDS in this poignant drama. *"There are many devastating ironies in Mr. Rabe's beautifully considered, piercingly clear-eyed work ... " –The NY Times. "With unsettling candor and disturbing insight, the play arouses pity and understanding of a troubling subject ... Rabe's provocative tale is an affirmation of dignity that rings clear and true." –Variety.* [6M, 1W] ISBN: 0-8222-1643-4

• **A DOLL'S HOUSE by Henrik Ibsen, adapted by Frank McGuinness. Winner of the 1997 Tony Award for best revival.** *"New, raw, gut-twisting and gripping. Easily the hottest drama this season." –USA Today. "Bold, brilliant and alive." –The Wall Street Journal. "A thunderclap of an evening that takes your breath away." –Time. "The stuff of Broadway legend." –Associated Press.* [4M, 4W, 2 boys] ISBN: 0-8222-1636-1

• **THE WAITING ROOM by Lisa Loomer.** Three women from different centuries meet in a doctor's waiting room in this dark comedy about the timeless quest for beauty -- and its cost. *" ... THE WAITING ROOM ... is a bold, risky melange of conflicting elements that is ... terrifically moving ... There's no resisting the fierce emotional pull of the play." –The NY Times. " ... one of the high points of this year's Off-Broadway season ... THE WAITING ROOM is well worth a visit." –Back Stage.* [7M, 4W, flexible casting] ISBN: 0-8222-1594-2

• **MR. PETERS' CONNECTIONS by Arthur Miller.** Mr. Miller describes the protagonist as existing in a dream-like state when the mind is "freed to roam from real memories to conjectures, from trivialities to tragic insights, from terror of death to glorying in one's being alive." With this memory play, the Tony Award and Pulitzer Prize-winner reaffirms his stature as the world's foremost dramatist. *" ... a cross between Joycean stream-of-consciousness and Strindberg's dream plays, sweetened with a dose of William Saroyan's philosophical whimsy ... CONNECTIONS is most intriguing ... Miller scholars will surely find many connections of their own to make between this work and the author's earlier plays." –The NY Times.* [5M, 3W] ISBN: 0-8222-1687-6

• **THE STEWARD OF CHRISTENDOM by Sebastian Barry.** A freely imagined portrait of the author's great-grandfather, the last Chief Superintendent of the Dublin Metropolitan Police. *"MAGNIFICENT ... the cool, elegiac eye of James Joyce's THE DEAD; the bleak absurdity of Samuel Beckett's lost, primal characters; the cosmic anger of KING LEAR ..." –The NY Times. "Sebastian Barry's compassionate imaging of an ancestor he never knew is among the most poignant onstage displays of humanity in recent memory." –Variety.* [5M, 4W] ISBN: 0-8222-1609-4

• **SYMPATHETIC MAGIC by Lanford Wilson. Winner of the 1997 Obie for best play.** The mysteries of the universe, and of human and artistic creation, are explored in this award-winning play. *"Lanford Wilson's idiosyncratic SYMPATHETIC MAGIC is his BEST PLAY YET ... the rare play you WANT ... chock-full of ideas, incidents, witty or poetic lines, scientific and philosophical argument ... you'll find your intellectual faculties racing." –New York Magazine. "The script is like a fully notated score, next to which most new plays are cursory lead sheets." –The Village Voice.* [5M, 3W] ISBN: 0-8222-1630-2

DRAMATISTS PLAY SERVICE, INC.
440 Park Avenue South, New York, NY 10016 212-683-8960 Fax 212-213-1539
postmaster@dramatists.com www.dramatists.com